This book is the gift of
THE CHURCH OF PERFECT LIBERTY
NORTH AMERICA
700 South Adams Street
Glendale, California 91205

The
Power *of*
Perfect Liberty

The
Power *of*
Perfect Liberty

Out of Japan:
A Creative
Breakthrough
in Humanity's
Quest for a
New Man in
a New Age

By Marcus Bach

PRENTICE-HALL, INC.
ENGLEWOOD CLIFFS, N.J.

The Power of Perfect Liberty   *Out of Japan: A Creative Breakthrough for a New Man in a New Age* by Marcus Bach

■ To Tokuharu Miki, founder and revelator of PL's basic Principles and Precepts, whose dedicated leadership has inspired the Perfect Liberty movement to become a power for good everywhere in the world. ■

Contents

The
Power *of*
Perfect Liberty

Chapter One

THE SONG
OF SELF

■ 1 ■

"YOU'RE HAPPY? What have you got to be happy
about?"

"I've got me!"

It was one of the shortest conversations I ever heard and
one of the most unforgettable.

I was in the quiet of the art gallery in the Biltmore Hotel
in Los Angeles. Here was this long-haired fellow with a
beard, looking twice his twenty years, scowling over a painting by Dai Chien. Apparently critical of what he saw, he
turned my way as if to say, "What's good about this?"

At that moment a long-haired, bright-eyed girl appeared
as if out of nowhere. She glided to the picture with a kind of
radiance and whispered half aloud, "Great, great!" Then she
caught herself, looked at the young man, and with a touch
of excitement said, "Don't you think it's great?" When he
shrugged gloomily, she shrugged, too, but with a laugh and
said, "Guess I'm just happy!"

11

It was then he mumbled, "You're happy? What have you got to be happy about?"

"I've got me!" she told him, as if the reason should be clear enough, and away she went with the step of a ballerina to view another work of art and then pass out of sight.

Long-haired girl, wherever you are, if you happen to read these words, tell me, "Are you by chance a follower of Perfect Liberty?"

She must have been because that, as far as PL people are concerned, is where happiness begins. It begins with the realization that, "I've got me!" In this one single respect we are all truly created equal. We have all been given an exclusive, individual Self. Our happiness, our state of being is as high as our surrender to this truth. The basic fact is that by the very nature of our existence we are one with the nature of God. *"I've got me!"*

■ 2 ■

This was my key to an understanding of this rapidly expanding Perfect Liberty movement, and I often thought about the art gallery incident during my months of PL research. Religion is my beat and for the past year I had been familiarizing myself with PL beliefs, PL followers, PL services and rituals no less than with its remarkable testimonials.

Now I was on my way to the PL headquarters in Tondabayashi, Japan. For thirteen hours the Boeing 747 would be my classroom for reading and studying the notes and books I had brought along and for calmly reflecting on the impact of this new religion in the life of modern man. It seemed to me at take-off from the Los Angeles airport that if a religion is not as modern as the incredible 747 and if it does not keep up with our swiftly changing times, it doesn't have a chance.

Consider the amazing change and progress that has taken place in the religion called Perfect Liberty. Ten years ago when I made a film on the emerging religions of Japan,* I did not even include this movement. I knew about it. I knew it was important, but I had no idea of its spectacular dynamic for growth. I had even dropped around to Tondabayashi City, about an hour's drive from Osaka, but we already had more footage of various Japanese festivals and faiths than we could use. So I merely toured the main buildings, took a quick look at the tremendous spurt of construction going on, but made no effort to get into the heart of it. After all, the grounds covered some twenty-five hundred acres. Where in America, or in the world, for that matter, would you find a religious tract to compare to that? How would PL ever utilize this vast expanse, I wondered, or fill it with buildings, to say nothing about people. I did notice an imposing golf course, and even in those days some people referred to PL as the "golf religion." But it was raining, the roads were muddy, and it was a dark, unphotogenic day.

Through the years, however, I kept hearing about PL and often ruefully admitted that I had all too quickly passed it up. When I lectured on religions there were frequent questions about PL and I was continually pressured by public interest and my innate quest to get up on it. I also encountered stories of healing miracles, of changed lives, and of the growing influence of PL until it was inevitable that I should find out just what was going on in this only Japanese-inspired religion with an English name.

Now the 747. Now the remembrance of the art gallery and "I've got me!" Now the prospect of being met in Tokyo by PL people and whisked away to Tondabayashi for a meeting with PL's Supreme Patriarch, Tokuchika Miki. Now the expectation of seeing for myself how dynamic the powerhouse of a new religion must be in order to impress Americans with the outreach of its strength.

I do my best thinking and my best reading in the air, and I've often noticed that the higher the altitude, the greater

* *Japan: Land of the Kami.*

13

my spiritual attitude! Our ranch house in the sky had now reached a cruising altitude of thirty-two thousand feet. I settled back and opened a book which I knew practically by heart: *The New Religions of Japan* by Harry Thomsen. In his chapter on PL he said,

> The seed of PL Kyodan (religion) was planted in 1912 with the founding of a new religion Tokumitsu-kyo, whose leader was an itinerant priest and spiritualist by name of Kanada Tokumitsu. One of Kanada's disciples was Miki Tokuharu, a Buddhist priest of the Obaku Zen sect. After the death of Kanada in 1919, Miki planted a shrub called himorogi at the place of Kanada's death. He worshipped it for five years in accordance with instructions given him by his master. At the end of the five years he claimed to have received the revelation promised by Kanada before his death.

> Miki then established a religion known as Hito no Michi (The Way of Man) in 1924. It was quite successful and is estimated to have had about one million believers by 1934. However, in 1937 the religion was prohibited by the government and Miki and many of his leaders were arrested on the charge of *lèse majesté*. In 1938 Miki Tokuharu died.

> His son Tokuchika was born in 1900. In later life he became the leader of Hito no Michi. This was not long before the 1945 Supreme Court verdict which upheld the earlier decision of lèse majesté and caused the disbanding of Hito no Michi. After the war in 1946, Tokuchika Miki and some leaders and members of the old group started Perfect Liberty Kyodan.

How easy and natural it sounded. How factual, how historic. Nothing about the suffering. Nothing about the spiritual bond that knit Kanada and Tokuharu Miki or of the latter's personal struggle, or of the mystic tie that gave Tokuchika Miki the power to reunite the scattered and persecuted people. But then, to catch the human interest is not necessarily the historian's assignment. That would be my

14

assignment. If PL turned out to be as important as my research up to now seemed to indicate, if Americans were actually finding something new and distinctive in this expanding faith, I would love to tell the story. I would describe the graphic encounter between Kanada and Tokuharu Miki (whose name at the time was actually Chogen Miki). I would tell how at their first meeting both men, despite their intensive experiences in the spiritual life, were still on a quest for deeper understanding. Approximately the same age, in their mid-forties, they met in an upper room in the modest Osaka dwelling where Kanada lived.

Chogen Miki at the time was a sick man, plagued by a persistent cough and suffering from facial spasms so severe he often covered his face with a scarf against the wind and cold. The doctors in his hometown had given him up as a consumptive. He was also fighting a battle with his own recalcitrant nature. He was in great physical pain when Kanada greeted him and asked him to write his name on a slip of paper. Chogen did so.

"You have a strong faith," Kanada said, turning the signature over and over in his hand. "You were happy once, though now you show unhappiness. You cannot forget many things about your hometown and the past."

"That is true," Chogen Miki admitted. "But since you have such powers, can you not cure me of my affliction, whatever it may be?"

Kanada had a faraway look in his eyes as if to convey what Chogen already knew: healing must come from within. A man must curb and bridle his nature. Chogen also knew that he was given to quick judgment, short temper and that despite his work as a priest he was still not a spiritually integrated man.

Kanada said quietly, "I can take your illness upon myself for a while."

"Can you do such a thing?"

"Surely I can."

Then Kanada began to cough, steadying his shaking breast

15

with his hands as Miki himself had done during his spells of coughing. Chogen became so deeply affected that he cried out, "Please stop it, if it causes you to suffer so much!"

"Do not worry," Kanada assured him in his apparent agony, "my cough will soon be cured. And so will yours."

So Chogen Miki began to look deeply within himself and was healed by virtue of the religious leader's mysterious power.

Such was the story and now when I thought of it I remembered testimonies that my PL friends had told me about *their* healings, how through prayer and the power of the present Patriarch, Tokuchika Miki, *they* had been cured of all sorts of diseases and helped in time of need.

What did I think of all this? Well, I remembered my visit several years ago with Padre Pio, a Catholic priest in Italy. He, too, took the sicknesses of others upon himself. So did Therese Neumann, the stigmatist of Konnersreuth, Germany, whom I had interviewed and written about in my book *The Circle of Faith*. They apparently had this talent or gift which PL referred to as the practice of *ofurikae*, a talent which passed from Kanada to Tokuharu Miki and on to Patriarch Tokuchika Miki whom I was to see.

What did I think of it? If a "Jumbo Jet" can speed through the skies at 670 miles per hour, carrying nearly four hundred passengers, and if the mind of man can create ships that fly to other planets, cannot the *spirit* of man demonstrate uncommon, supernormal healing talents for the benefit of humanity? I had found too much evidence in my years of research to doubt these things.

I understood how Chogen Miki must have felt when he left Kanada's presence after his first visit and returned to his duties as a Zen priest. I could see how he could never get it out of his mind that a spiritual demonstration had taken place and that even though this was considered unnatural in Zen, it was natural according to the nature of God and man.

Chogen Miki's vocation as priest was never the same. He performed his duties and made his meditations and continued to develop the spirit of self-detachment. He left the priesthood at intervals and took up secular work, but the memory of Kanada would not leave him. Nor could he forget that Kanada had said to him, "Come work with me. Some day I will establish my own religious movement. What do you think, Mr. Miki?"

Inevitably the day came when Chogen Miki rapped once more at the door of Kanada's newly established house of religion called *Tokumitsu-kyo*.

"You know, Mr. Miki," Kanada said quietly, "yesterday when I passed the Tetsuganji Temple where you once lived the thought struck me that you would come to me today."

Chogen Miki was deeply impressed with this evidence of thought transference. "I would like to dedicate my life to helping people," he said with emotion.

That was how the bond between the two men began and how through prayer and service to others their spiritual partnership was eventually sealed. Kanada gave Chogen the spiritual name of Tokuharu and to Chogen's eldest son Akisada, who was in his teens and already engaged in religious study, he conferred the name Tokuchika, the man who was now the Patriarch.

This was how the PL story began, and as this first fragment passed through my mind I took from my briefcase a gold-bordered parchment on which in artistic lettering was written, "The Reverend Tokuchika Miki, Supreme Patriarch of PL Kyodan requests the pleasure of your company . . . on Wednesday the eighth of April . . . at ten o'clock . . . at the headquarters . . . in Tondabayashi City. . . ."

■ 2 ■

I often have a feeling on a long plane trip that we are all players in a cosmic drama. We travel together for a little while, scarcely knowing one another; we exchange glances, think our own thoughts, keep the depth of feeling to ourselves, and always have more in common than we will admit. Our sense of wonder at the magic carpet that carries us so effortlessly, our awareness that destiny has made us fellow passengers for a while, each with his own destination in mind, our sense of mortality and immortality, too—these are our innermost emotions and just now they brought me back to the art gallery and what I have called the Song of Self.

PL has a remarkable way of making this particularization of self real and graphic. It teaches that the creative power of the universe reveals itself in many a 747 or a golf course, a successful business enterprise or a career of any kind, a skyscraper or a piece of calligraphy, a leaf or a forest, a grain of sand or a mountain, a man, a woman, a child; whatever living thing it is, it must, in order to find its true form, get rid of its ego. Why? Because the true self within each of us must have perfect liberty for its expression. The ego does not free the true self, as some mistakenly believe; it enslaves it. Get rid of your ego, says PL. Set the true self (your divine nature) free and it will literally burst out in a vivid demonstration of the glory of *being*.

It cannot do otherwise. Its expression is its life and its life is its expression. If there is one thing God must do, it is express Himself, and each of us is His radiant living center. In everything, through everything, an irresistible creative power continues to unfold and reveal itself. Ego-free, says PL, you are that power particularized.

I had been told that huge crowds, hundreds of thousands of people, come to the PL headquarters at Tondabayashi to witness the greatest, most spectacular display of fireworks in all the world. On August 7, the date of the passing of the First Patriarch, Tokuharu Miki, the sky is filled with lights and sounds in a kaleidoscope of color that dazzles the mind. What do people find in this? Entertainment, beauty, love of life? A remembrance that Tokuharu Miki said, "Do not

18

grieve over my passing but celebrate it with fireworks in the sky"? All of these and something more. In the burst of these radiant rainbows against the night, in the intricate formations of flickering beauty, is a symbol of God expressing Himself. He cannot help it. It is His way. As the fireworks must explode and show forth their hidden glory, so must God. When people see this spectacle and gaze at it spellbound, something says to them: you are that power particularized.

Every great world religion has tried to describe this truth. Every great teacher has hoped to get this idea awakened in his people. Every poet and artist has sought to express it and most of us have one time or other thought about it. Now along comes PL and says, "Religion is an experience in happiness! Through Perfect Liberty we will help you find the way!"

It was "the way" that interested me, for it is one thing for a religion to make claims and quite another thing to demonstrate these claims in life. That was what my notes were all about: case histories reported by PL people whom I had interviewed.

Selecting one at random, I found the testimony of a young woman who said, "It used to be that everything in life was out of timing. I was usually at the wrong place at the wrong time. I did not have the good luck that other people had. I worried about the past and about the future. I felt I had to worry or I would not be a good mother. The more I worried the worse things went. The worse things went, the angrier I got. The angrier I got, the worse things went.

"I came into PL because I needed help. That is why many people come into it. The PL ministers are always ready to help. They have a way of knowing what a person needs. If they do not know, the Patriarch does and he has taken an oath to help us.

"What happened to me in PL? The ego that was once so important to me was put out of the way. That was the first

19

thing. A new feeling about life came to me through the prayers and the teaching. I learned to express myself, and I no longer had after-feelings or after-thoughts. I began to live in the present. The moment that became important was *now*. Worry is a negative power. Happiness is positive. When I found this way of life, I came in tune with things and now my timing is always right. Now the world is on my side and people are rooting for me instead of against me."

I turned from this testimony to look out of the plane at the brilliant horizon line, a crimson thread between sky and sea. Actually one could not tell where the earth ended and the heavens began and that is how it must have been with this woman when she observed that, "When you are in tune, the timing is always right." Like the timing of a plane or the plane of life. The perfectly timed hum of the engines, the razor-sharp tone of absolute balance, the flawless flight of a clipper ship in tune with the laws of aerodynamics and space. The "Jumbo Jet" singing the Song of Self.

■ 3 ■

There is a saying in America, "The environment you live in is the environment that lives in you." PL goes further. It says the environment you live in *is* you. To quote it precisely as stated in PL's Twenty-one Precepts, "Our whole environment is the mirror of our mind!"

This is a deep philosophical truth. Many philosophies insist that the physical world is really not an independently existing object, but that everything we see and hear is merely a projection of ideas existing in mind. PL proposes that the natural world is like a mirror in which we see the reflection of what we believe the world to be. Like the young man and woman in the art gallery: the bearded youth looked at the picture and scowled; the long-haired girl called it great. Each saw the painting through an inner eye. Imagine the universe for a moment as your art gallery and listen once more to the PL precept, "Our whole environment is the mirror of our mind!"

Look out the window of a plane at the wisps of clouds or at the ocean beneath and they do seem to say, "We are what you see within yourself. We are your moods and your thoughts, but still we have our own identity." Your world is the mirror image of yourself. Look at all of nature, at the passengers going with you through life, at your job, your surroundings, your family, your friends, and see them as God-particularized-and-harmonized-in-life even as *you*. That is why PL says that the light by which you see your world comes from within yourself.

You are the place of beginning, the focal point. Stand straight and free in Perfect Liberty, not in body only, but in mind. Within the physical is the spiritual, within the spiritual is the universal, within the universal is *you*, which is the nature of God.

Since PL's teaching that "Our whole environment is the mirror of our mind!" is found in one form or other in all major religions and lurks in most of the world's philosophies, why did it strike me so forcefully when I ran across it in PL? Perhaps because of its overtone of freedom, its continual insistence that we cannot truly realize our innermost manifestation unless we are free.

That is certainly a typically American point of view, in fact, the very heart of democracy. No wonder PL appeals to our people! After all, we grew up on the Christian axiom that, "Ye shall know the Truth and the Truth shall make you *free*." PL was simply saying, "Why not believe it and live it?"

Most of us grew up on songs of liberty and freedom. Most of us memorized Walt Whitman's lines, "I celebrate myself, and sing myself! What I assume you shall assume! Every atom belonging to me belongs to you!"

All imaginative poets and all religions were in agreement

21

at this central point: *The individual is a manifestation of God.* Buddhism, Hinduism, Shinto, Christianity—these and others had already told me that freedom is indispensable in order to properly sing the Song of Self.

PL's agreement with all great religions was part of PL's appeal. It was the first to admit that most of its teachings have their pre-teachings in other, older faiths. When it said that the more you try to be someone else the less you are happy and free, and the less you are free the less you fulfill your true role in life, it was a statement both old and new. When it warned us that the more we are governed by our ego, the less we are our true Self, that, too, had ancient roots as well as a fresh, contemporary application.

But certainly, Patriarch Miki had a new idea when he made it clear that he did not want his followers to become carbon copies of himself. In most religions the leaders ask their adherents to conform to their examples and use their doctrines as models against which to measure their perfection. Patriarch Miki, or Oshieoya, as he is known in PL, asks his followers to be themselves, for it is in being that we become and it is in becoming that we discover the reason for our existence.

I remembered the feeling of kinship that came to me when I first read some of Oshieoya's writings. He wrote many things I secretly believed, and they went through my mind as the jet spread its wings ever further across the Pacific. "It should be a way of life," said the Patriarch, "to adapt oneself to one's surroundings, to merge into them, at any moment, in any given situation. Man who is unable to do so is the obstinate one and unable to adjust to Divine Acts. Such a one is a thoughtless being who knows nothing but to cling to his own ego."

How true. What if the pilot were to say, "I will not adapt to the laws of flying or to the instruments or to the flight pattern"?

The assumption in Perfect Liberty is that you must know

the rules before you take liberty with the rules. Happiness is not a matter of libertarianism because libertarianism can itself be a chain that keeps you from being free. Before you take liberties, know that you can be trusted with them.

A PL follower shared a most interesting story with me about the liberty he asserted in giving away his last dollar. It was some weeks before payday and he had many bills that had to be met. He had his PL offering box well filled with his donations for the PL church. PL people call this method of giving, "*hosho*," a form of love-offering. For a moment this man was tempted to use the *hosho* money and not go to the meeting on the prescribed day for the Thanksgiving Service, held on the twenty-first of each month. Why not take the *hosho* money and use it for his own purpose? Struggling with his decision, he remembered the words of the Patriarch, "Win by giving up! You must give away what you have to multiply your material rewards."

The PL member turned the words over in his mind and decided to take the saying literally. Instead of robbing his offering box, he added his last dollar to it and took it all to the church. *Hosho*, selflessly given. Three days later he received through the mail an unexpected payment from a friend who years ago had borrowed money from him and had never repaid it. Now it came in perfect timing. What more evidence did he need to prove the truth of Miki's words, "Win by giving up!" or how could he ever again doubt the workability of the *hosho* law?

"Happiness," Patriarch Miki said, "is concerned with total character and total activity of man. If a man molds this total activity of character in life, it must be beautiful and pleasant in the widest sense of the word. Get rid of your ego. Win by giving up!"

He was saying what I had learned convincingly by way of my research. Faith works where you work at your faith. The law of giving is the law of God. Learn the law so that you can be free of the law.

When you have a sure and deeply rooted religious belief, you can enjoy and appreciate the luxury of *all* faiths. The more you are devoted to your own family the more you can enjoy all families and the better is your understanding of family life. The greater your love for the country of your birth the more meaningful all countries become. It is then you can understand the deeper meaning of patriotism. You are free only when you give up. You are happy when you know that "I've got me!" means that everyone else has his "me" and for him it is equally as precious as yours.

Once the Patriarch told a group of followers, "Walk with sincerity whatever your road." That was a basic theme in my years of research. I had always said, "All roads that lead to God are good." At times I was severely criticized for this. "What do you mean?" people said. "How can there be more than one road?" They did not understand. They did not understand that every life is a road to God, and a road from God, too. In fact, every life is *the* road. That was why I felt a warmth for the Patriarch when he said, "Walk with sincerity whatever your road."

"And go with faith whatever your flight!" I said as the noonday sun struck the giant wings of the jet with a silvery touch. How exciting the world and how marvelous the quest!

Just now it seemed to me that God offered to every one of us a choice between perfect liberty and enslavement. Between these two conditions most people vacillate. All PL was saying is that an individual should choose the better way, the freedom way. If we cling to our ego, our ego enslaves us. If we set our mind on wealth, wealth is our master. If we think only of making good in the world, ambition rules us. If we have too many possessions, we are possessed. If we accept the fact of living in turmoil and struggle, this soon becomes our way of life. If a man's mind is not in order, the more knowledge he has, the greater his confusion. We must get rid of our captives before we can be truly free.

Happiness means balance in life. It is always close at hand, waiting in the present moment, riding with us at our side in the eternal Now. It is as if God were saying, "What do you truly want? What is your deepest desire? Take it, pay for it, and go your way!"

Perfect Liberty. Total happiness. How simple it all seemed at this high altitude! How simple it all was! As simple as fireworks against the sky. As simple as the PL follower who took his *hosho* to the Thanksgiving Service. As simple as a long-haired girl in an art gallery who said, "I've got me!"

"I've got me. And *you* have *you*. And we are all in life together as manifestations of the living God.

What more do we need to begin to sing our Song of Self?

Chapter Two

LIFE IS ART

■ 1 ■

THE MAN NEXT to me in our 747, who was getting off in Honolulu, was good enough to let me sort out my PL notes and do my writing without being too inquisitive about my activity. He had, however, drawn out of me that I was on a mission to Japan. Then he put on his reading glasses and settled down with a copy of *Newsweek*. After several hours in flight, he nudged me and handed me the open copy of the magazine.

"If you are going to Nippon," he said, "better read this."

He laid the magazine in my lap and a headline blazed up at me: JAPAN—SALESMAN TO THE WORLD! A byline, equally arresting, quoted the statement of a U.S. oil executive: "Wake up, America! And watch the Rising Sun!"

I read the account, the gist of which was that Japan is growing and gaining on all the world in the fields of industry and culture. The thesis had it that Japanese influence would dominate the twenty-first century. The prediction was that if its present dedication to creativity, research and plain hard work continued for another ten or fifteen years, the Japanese could conceivably "inherit the earth."

What the article failed to mention was that Japan's new religions, which I had been reporting on for the past ten years, had revolutionized the spiritual and cultural scene and literally turned people on with a new dynamic in their relationship with God and man.

It struck me as more than mere chance that this fellow passenger should have handed the magazine to me. Surely this was more than serendipity. It was also more than a coincidence that my sheaf of notes on PL should momentarily be lying beneath the news story of Japan's industrial and social growth. To me it was symbolic, for I was convinced that the soil out of which Japan's skills and creativity grew was spiritual. It was my impression that PL and other contemporary faiths were major factors in undergirding the industrial revolution, and I was anxious to get Patriarch Miki's views on this. At any rate, I had been pleading for a long time that American religions take a look at the tremendous dimensions of inner dedication in this land of the Rising Sun and find out what is happening in a country where work is a form of worship and where God is not far off, but excitingly near.

I put the magazine aside. On the very top of my PL notes was a manila folder on which I had written, "Life Is Art!" Beneath this I had put a P.S. "This may be PL's secret weapon." It was my way of reminding myself of the first time, nearly a year ago, when I read PL's Twenty-one Precepts and was struck by the phrase, LIFE IS ART, at the head of the list.

Inside the folder were my notes.

> "The wonderful thing about PL," a follower told me, "is that it helped me solve my problems and showed me the way to go."

Question: How did it help? How did it point the way?

"To begin with, it told me that LIFE IS ART. The moment I came into PL I became an artist."

As far as I was concerned, that *was* PL's greatest beginning. It *was* its secret constructive weapon. In fact, my definition of a PL follower was simply this: *A PL person is one who has discovered and lives by the principle that Life Is Art.*

Invariably I was asked, "What's new about that? Isn't that what every religion teaches?"

It would seem so. It seemed that way to me. I had a feeling that even the phrase, "Life Is Art," was one I had heard over and over long before I ever heard of PL. But the more I thought about it, the clearer it became that for some strange reason these three simple words, "Life Is Art," were unique and special. Whenever I asked myself where I *had* heard them, I was at a loss for an explanation. As in so many of PL's teachings, the truths were old but the presentation and application of them were strikingly new.

I had often heard about life being *compared* to art. since my earliest school days phrases like, "Art is long and time is fleeting," "Art consists of bringing something into existence," and "Art is the path of the creator to his work," had been part of my learning process. In my study of Buddhism I learned that "Man is fashioned by his thinking," and in Christianity I was taught the parable of the potter and the clay. All were clearly hints on the art of living.

But when I heard PL's terse and graphic phrase, "Life Is Art," everything connected with my life was suddenly challenged to take on an artistic touch, and instantly the total outlook on life took on a new perspective.

"Come to think of it," I said, "I *am* the artist! I am the master craftsman shaping my existence from the cradle to the grave. I wield the tools, dream the dreams, see the visions, draw the plans, take the time, do the work in everything I say and think every moment of the day. As a sculptor takes his raw material and begins to realize the ideal, or idealize the real, as a painter takes his brush and gives form to his creative idea, so in total life I am the artist!"

PL pinned it down and gave it power. PL made it logical and direct. "The moment I came into PL I became an artist," said the man in my memo.

No matter who you are or what you are, the raw material of every life encounter is the stuff with which you must work. From now on everything that happens—sickness, bad breaks, good breaks, joy, success—everything challenges your artistry.

Trouble at home? Life is Art.

You have been unjustly accused? Life is Art.

A loved one has died? Life is Art.

You ran into a bad situation? Life is Art.

You are enjoying a moment of triumph? Life is Art.

What kind of an artist are you?

Here was actually something new, a new idea, a new art form. In these modern days of Funk art, Junk art, Pop art, Mod art, all kinds of art, here was *Life Art,* arising from within oneself.

Along came PL. Its Patriarch insisted that art in life, as art in any medium, must always be original. "Imitation is not true art," he said. "It may be a true imitation, but it is not true art."

If you must use an old idea or an old art form or an old concept, at least give it your own original twist. This has nothing to do with religion as an institution, it has to do with religion as *life.* Life is Art.

Again I was struck by an analogy. Japanese industry, American industry were forging ahead, sparked by such slogans as "Research is the key to tomorrow," "Better living through creativity," "Keep in tune with the Now generation." Could religion afford to remain static? Could the church insist on walking backward into yesterday?

30

The greatest art is the art of becoming.

The perfect artist, said PL, is God. He gives us the best example of creative talent by making everything different and original. He uses the same basic stuff of life, but fashions everything to be uniquely distinctive. From sea urchin to man, He gives each its own individuality. Never the same sunrise. Never the same cloud formation. Never the same scenes out of the windows of a moving plane. Never the same personality among your fellow passengers. Never the same voices. For millions of years, locked within the limitless mind of God, new expressions have been released as if He simply *had* to make room for more.

Locked within us, waiting to be expressed, are similar potentials. Everyone has them in abundance. Kanada in his upper room. Tokuharu Miki under the *sakaki* tree His son, Patriarch Miki, in the PL compound. I in the jet You wherever you may be. We cannot listen to the whisper of God or to the still small voice within our heart without hearing them say, "Life Is Art!"

■ 2 ■

As the plaintive murmur of the mammoth ship sang about its own artistry, I had a hunch that if PL could get its "Life Is Art" message across to our Western world it would stop people in their tracks. It could move through America and change lives as surely as if it had a magic wand. Whether it would do it or not was, of course, up to PL. Whether it would inspire questing Americans to "look to the Rising Sun" was also up to the power of Perfect Liberty. The fact that PL was the only Japanese religion with an English name already hinted that it had a greater world in mind than just Japan.

"Life Is Art," as I had noted in my memo, was indeed the beginning. PL's second precept was an amplification. It made clear that the way to truly live as though Life is Art

31

is to "Look upon your whole life as a continuous succession of self-expressions." This, too, seemed like something I had been hearing all my life, but, again, PL pinned it down. You could not read this second precept about life's being a continuous series of self-expressions without asking yourself, "How am I doing as an artist?"

As a writer I had the idea that my self-expression was *not* a continuous succession. I was of the opinion that my artistry revealed itself only when I was writing. Whenever I raised my eyes to my library shelf and saw copies of my books all neatly bound and jacketed, I said, "Ah, there is my self-expression!" When I found articles of mine in magazines, I told myself, "There is your self-expression." I honestly thought that writing was my total field of creativity, just as you may feel that your particular vocation or profession, your housework or office work or whatever your job may be, is *your* complete self-expression. This is only part of it.

PL cues us in on the fact that the thoughts we think, the words we speak, the things we do, our off-job as well as our on-job moments, our leisure, play, fun, joy, sorrow, struggle, success, our everything is "a continuous succession of self-expressions." That is why "Life Is Art" is the beginning, the challenge of a new life, and the *succession* of self-expressions is the process by which this artistry is achieved.

It finally occurred to me—at thirty-two thousand feet— that the most significant of all books I could ever write was the living narrative of me, total me, written not on paper but in my day-by-day experiences. That would be the book that would one day judge me and give me an idea of my artistry. That would be the one that truly bore my signature, my complete and unadulterated authorship. Such is the case with every individual. In this respect we are all PL people whether we are PL followers or not.

Among my notes was an interview I had with a PL member. When I asked him how things were going, he said,

"Very good. In fact, just very, very good!"

I shared with him a pet theory of mine that life moves in cycles. We have our good cycles and our moments when we feel we are at the bottom of the wheel. I suggested to him that a person should by rights make the most of his good cycles and "lay low" during the bad ones. He listened politely, then shook his head. "I'll tell you how it is with me since I came into PL," he said. "My good cycles are good, but my bad cycles are good, too. And if life is a wheel as you say, well then, I am always going forward!"

The Patriarch would have agreed. "All outcomes in life are Divine Acts," he once said. "All things in nature present themselves to us as material for self-expression and by free utilization of this material we become creative and learn the meaning of peace."

This means that every life, like every path, may have unexpected turns and hills to climb and valleys to go through. But what PL says loud and clear is that these challenges can be utilized for growth and may actually prove to be short cuts to self-realization. Difficulties may be blessings in disguise. They may be warnings from God which, if rightly heeded, will avert future difficulties.

To fully understand the precept that "Life Is Art," PL asks Westerners to learn a new word: *Mishirase*. Once heard, *Mishirase* is never forgotten. While it has no exact equivalent in the English language, PL defines it as "divine warnings," and in my notes I referred to it as "our deviation from the divine norm." This becomes clear if we refer back to the PL belief that, "Our whole environment is the mirror of our mind." When we deviate from the fact that illness, misfortune and the like are caused by an over-ego emphasis within ourselves, then we are confronted by *Mishirase*. When we blame everything on outside influences instead of examining our inner self, the true reflection of life is blurred. The breath of our ego beclouds the mirror.

Mishirase is one way of saying that we must recognize our deviation from the divine norm.

How do we correct this? The best correction, the best antidote according to PL, involves another interesting word: *Mioshie*. This word, too, catches our imagination and sticks in our mind, for if *Mishirase* is wrong thinking and deviation, then *Mioshie* is the technique for right thinking and a return to solid logic and reason.

According to the PL glossary, *Mioshie* involves divine instructions and divine teachings. This means that a person with a *Mishirase* experience may go to his local minister and through analysis and guidance receive a *Mioshie*, that is, expert help and counsel. When the local PL minister feels the need of deeper insight than he can give, he consults the Patriarch and receives a *Mioshie* directly from headquarters based on the mystical enlightenment with which the Patriarch is endowed.

The logic of PL comes through clearly at this point. In writing about "Life Is Art," Miki said,

> People tend to say, "I am the best judge of myself, I know what is right and wrong for me better than anyone else." But is that true? The fact is, no matter how hard and sincerely you try, you have many faults, shortcomings and wrong-doings which you cannot even detect, much less overcome. Then, what should you do?

> Think of the would-be golfer or artist or musician. What does he do when he wishes to develop his potentialities? Naturally he seeks the advice and assistance of a coach or teacher.

> Well, then, just so you too must be mature and frank enough to listen to great teachers of religion if you are truly interested in a better life for yourself and your loved ones. Material wealth does not assure you happiness any more than an expensive set of golf clubs is a guarantee to play a good game.

Likewise, knowledge alone is insufficient to find the answers to the inquiries of man.

The PL religion teaches you the correct mental attitude in accordance with the Divine Universal Scheme. In other words, we guide each individual personally, according to his environment and character so that he can live a full, happy and unique life and be in perfect harmony with the rules of the universe. Life Is Art.

Mishirase and *Mioshie* represent the clearinghouse of the mind and the rebirth of the spirit. PL's commentary on the Twenty-one Precepts makes it clear that regardless of the religion one follows, if one lives with a wrong mind, a mind with various bad propensities, *Mishirase* will visit you. If you live with a right mind regardless of your religious affiliation, good will be your reward. It is not a matter of belonging to this church or that, it is a matter of the proper mental and spiritual approach.

If, however, you become a member of PL, you will be taught precisely what each *Mishirase* means and you will be shown the proper *Mioshie* to assure effective results. Some people take their troubles to psychoanalysts, ministers, priests or holy men in various faiths, others go to spiritual healers, counselors, astrologers and all sorts of therapists. PL people go to PL leaders or teachers and this is one reason for the integrated strength and growth of the movement. Its followers believe that PL has the most responsible techniques and is continually improving its methods in the total healing and unification of body, mind and spirit.

One phase of this is research in the psychosomatic field as well as in medicine generally. I had been told that startling things were happening in medical research at Tondabayashi. In its ultra-modern hospital, staff members are also PL ministers, providing spiritual guidance in connection with conventional medical care. "Due to mutual trust between doctors and patients," said PL, "the percentage and speed of recovery are amazingly high." From organic to functionary ills, from deep physical problems to equally deep psychological distresses, the keynote of "Life Is Art" related to *Mishirase* and *Mioshie* evidently provided positive steps toward a higher artistry.

I was anxious to see what I would find, for until now most of my information had been hearsay. And naturally when I heard reports about "a million case records of *Mioshie*," and claims that "PL has the most computerized approach to healing in the world," I had my doubts. Still, on an elementary basis I felt I knew what *Mishirase* and *Mioshie* were all about. For example, a friend of mine, who had never heard a word about PL, was what the doctors called "accident prone." If there was anything that could happen to a man in the way of getting hurt, it happened to him. When getting into a car, he would invariably bang his head. If there was anything to stumble over, he would find it. When I attended a dinner in his home, he cut his finger while slicing the roast.

One day when he caught his heel in a broken curb he went back and kicked the curb so hard he sprained a toe on the other foot. I said to him, "Don't kick the curb, kick yourself." We had a talk. I told him what I had learned about PL's theories about *Mishirase* and *Mioshie*, sharing with him the theory that we have within ourselves an unconscious tendency toward blaming others when, in fact, we should examine ourselves. We have a habit of fixing the responsibility on objects outside ourselves when it is actually a deviation from the quietude within that causes us to hurry, worry, become impatient and develop rash tendencies that eventually induce sickness, pain, accidents and all sorts of discomforts.

Somehow this got through to him and actually changed his attitude. Without any other effort on his part except his determination to hold the proper mental state and get his improper ego out of the way, he developed a certain art of living.

And I could see how the *Mishirase-Mioshie* equation could be applied to any number of stubborn psychological problems, and to equally deep-seated tendencies which have held us captive because of our failure to see that they might actually be logical starting points for spiritual growth. This much of a personal testimony I was ready to give to the elementary value of *Mioshie* and a step toward the liberation of self.

■ 3 ■

"Life Is Art" kept reminding me that all areas of experience are interlocking and interrelated. If we improve our activity in one field, say in the way we walk or talk or pace ourselves, this improvement is immediately reflected in the way we do our job, the way we deal with our clients, our family and our life generally. Patriarch Miki said, "It is only in the process of working and looking for the highest stage devotedly that we express and mold our true and total self. When an expression has individuality, it has value. When it lacks individuality, it has no value worthy of art. To express oneself fully it is necessary to subordinate the ego."

While I realized it was not a true analogy to compare an airplane to a living being, the 747 tempted me to draw a comparison in the light of the Patriarch's words. A mechanism such as a plane does not have the soul of a man, but it has the soul of a mechanism. It may not be self-directive as is a person, but the subtle inter-association of its parts was, for me, in this moment of flight, an analogy I could not resist.

Hidden in this miracle of aeronautics which was transporting a small city full of people (361 of us) through the ocean of space at 625 miles an hour, concealed in this intricate and fascinating anatomy of engineering, lay miles of hidden wiring, mazes of technical devices, intricate networks of electronic arteries and nerves, capillaries of gears and gadgets; four million parts, to be exact, all functioning flawlessly, all synchronized and synthesized in the common cause of raising its occupants to what I have called a new spiritual altitude. What a parable of the subordination of the ego! What a vision of the total self! "I live," says the PL creed, "for the joy and satisfaction of an artistic life!"

If one part of that puzzle of wires and millions of moving parts in the plane should lose its artistry the total effect would be impaired. If it ever forgot that life is a continuous succession of self-expressions it would be just too bad for all of us passengers, as it is too bad for the world if society forgets the value of its individual units, and it is too bad for the individual if he fails to realize how his inner life is interrelated. PL feels this way about the functional factors in all existence. It aims at the artistic integration within the individual, within family and social groups, within nations and within humanity. Only when there is artistry throughout can there be the "great peace" PL so often talks about.

"When my total self is manifested completely in my action and expressions," says Tokuchika Miki, "when the three facets of art—mental activity, inner response, and outer expression—are unified, then everything is stirred by the power of 'Life Is Art'."

I used the illustration of the jet. The Patriarch once used the analogy of "Man and horse in one body." I knew what he meant because not long ago in Vienna I witnessed the rare artistry of the Spanish Riders, the world's greatest equestrian attraction. They demonstrated with flawless skill the art of man and horse becoming inseparably one.

Watching this hypnotic performance I became unaware of rider and unaware of steed. All I saw was art in motion.

Here was complete effacement of man-ego and horse-ego, and a perfect demonstration of a non-ego spiritual experience. As horse and rider were absolutely blended, so we are urged to become so absorbed and unified in our successions of self-expression that the God-nature and our nature become indivisibly one.

What would my meeting with Patriarch Miki be like? That remained to be seen. I have visited many religious leaders: two popes, two jungle doctors, a walking saint in India, a Zen master in Mandalay, a Baha'i guardian in Haifa, and so on. One thing that impressed me and humbled me was their egolessness, their sensitive art of life. Their presence was predominantly spiritual and drew me into a mystical moment of that awareness. Our minds harmonized. Our instant of life became one. During my final meeting with a Japanese religious leader, Tenko-san, it would have been almost sacrilegious to have said good-bye or *aufwiedersehen* or *sayonara*. All we could do was bow to each other and then clasp hands and quietly affirm that there is no parting in spirit.

True art must be expressed. The plane must function cooperatively. The book of self must be written. *Mishirase* must be understood. *Mioshie* must be applied. The horse and rider must become one. The ego must be effaced. When this is done everyone feels it and knows it. To live totally is to unify mind, spirit and body in art.

There is art in discovering the truth about yourself, art in dealing with the seemingly inevitable, art in every walk of life, art in the entire succession of self-expressions. The indestructible dancer, Fred Astaire, once said, "There is even an artistic way of picking up a garbage can."

Unite the artistic and the functional and you are close to the secret of Perfect Liberty. "If you lay out a garden," says a Japanese axiom, "let the proportion be at least four of beauty to six of utility." And if you build a jet, let it be an expression of aesthetic wonder and mechanical perfection.

39

Let there be harmony between man and the creative spirits, for, as PL says, the perfect way of man is perfect understanding of the way of the gods.

Our whole environment is the mirror of our mind.

Man's true self is revealed when his ego is effaced.

Your whole life is a continuous succession of self-pression.

Life Is Art.

Chapter Three

MAKOTO

■ 1 ■

AFTER A STOP in Honolulu, our astroliner was again soaring effortlessly to its highway in the sky. I got to thinking how much of my life has been spent in the kind of research that was taking me to Tondabayashi. By plane and train, by ship and dugout canoe, by car, pedicab, tonga and on foot, I had followed the spoors of living faiths, all precious to those who found them meaningful, all of them meaningful to me.

There was hardly a religious movement I had not sought to interpret, and there was none for which I did not feel an empathic fellowship. One thing all earthlings have in common is the quest, and it had become a creed with me that wherever man lives man worships. The spirit of God is coded in us.

At some point in life we are like Kanada, taking the sufferings of others upon ourselves. Somewhere along the way

41

we are like Tokuharu Miki meditating beneath the *sakaki* tree. There comes a time when, like Tokuchika Miki, we build upon and add to the contemporary significance of what we and others have so richly found.

Apparently Patriarch Miki's views regarding world religions were in accord with mine. In most of my twenty books my basic theme was that the various faiths are dialects by which man speaks to God and God to man. That seemed to be Oshieoya's belief. He once wrote,

"What is human life? What is the nature of God? What is right and wrong? How can we find peace of mind? Is there a sure way to happiness? What happens after death? From time immemorial, mankind has pondered these questions. Many great religions have emerged to offer answers and to give spiritual illumination to these basic inquiries. Therefore, it is not surprising to discover that the great religions of the world are quite alike in their deepest aspirations."

As the sturdy wings of the plane relaxed with weightless ease, I had to admit that the more I read of Miki's philosophy the more comfortable I felt about our forthcoming meeting. It was good to know that we had many conclusions in common. The thought was reassuring but it puzzled me, too. While truth is truth wherever found, I nonetheless really thought I had arrived at some spiritual breakthroughs which were strictly my own as, for example, my deep-seated conviction that religion is not an opinion but an experience; that we understand people best when we understand what they believe and so on. Furthermore, it again occurred to me that what I had discovered through years of travel and research had evidently been revealed to men like Patriarch Miki and others by the simple or not-so-simple process of enlightenment.

According to the history of PL, after Tokuharu Miki experienced his spiritual attainment following five years of special devotion, he recognized this same degree of consciousness in his son Tokuchika who was then thirty-six years of age. This was in 1936, the year in which Japan and Germany signed the anti-Comintern pact. In other words, the trend throughout the world was toward troubled times during the year (1936) when the leadership of Hito-no-Michi passed from Tokuharu Miki (known as Kyoso or Founder) to Tokuchika Miki with the title of Oshieoyo or Patriarch. All of this was just prior to the charges of *lèse majesté*, so-called offenses against the Imperial regime. Governments everywhere were fearful and jealous of their powers and those who questioned the divine absolutism of any earthly ruler were naturally suspect. Accusations and persecutions were common against many emerging religions in Japan prior to and during the war.

As a result, Tokuharu Miki died in prison where Tokuchika himself was forced to remain until MacArthur's momentary rule and authority exonerated him of all charges and established his innocence. True freedom of religion finally came to Japan in 1946 and "Perfect Liberty" was chosen as the title for the Hito-no-Michi faith, as if to indicate that when you reach the state of PL you are at last liberated from worry, suffering, misfortune, hate, conflict and hostility.

You might say that when you arrive at a consciousness of Perfect Liberty you are finally out of prison, or you might also compare PL to the freedom and wonder of a liberty-loving jet that plys the sky.

■ 2 ■

I had with me in the plane a tape recording that gave me one of the best insights into PL at this stage of my research. Firmly fixed in my cassette recorder, it represented the enthusiastic testimony and the expert opinions of an American business executive of San Francisco, who had be-

43

come a convert to PL and one of its foremost American interpreters. I had met many converts to the faith and while they all had the indoctrination of PL teachings in common there was something quite uncommon about Donald Steele. For one thing, many of his points of view bore so closely on what I had found in my research and written about in my books that I felt a kinship with him and had persuaded him to put his impressions on my cassette recorder.

It is quite a world when you stop to think about it. Here you are flying at nearly the speed of sound in a ship that weighs nearly a million pounds, yet seems as light and graceful as a sea gull. You hold a small black box to your ear, press a button and listen to a voice coming from a razor-thin ribbon on which the words are invisibly etched in electronic hieroglyphics. You close your eyes and relive again the moments when these words were captured by a microphone more sensitive than the human ear.

So I listened while Don Steele's recorded message spoke to me: "There must be thousands of people like you and me in America, tens of thousands, whose lives are on a quest and who could find instantly what you and I have looked for and tried to find by years of study and reading. Instant discovery could be theirs as instantly as it was mine."

As I listened to these words a profile of the man returned to mind. He was a strapping, athletic type, a man in middle age with a background career in radio and TV, a singing star and, for a time, a columnist. Now he was president of the San Francisco office of the International Public Relations Company, an around-the-world network founded by a Japanese, Taiji Kohara. Square-jawed, dynamic, confident, he could not be mistaken for anything but a down-to-earth realist in the usual sense, but even during my first meeting with him I was struck by a strange softness and sensitive insight through which a spiritual drift in his conversation drew me more and more into a relationship with something beyond the common values by which we measure material success.

I met him on several occasions. He had a charismatic quality, a confidence that a divine order runs through life and that we can never live apart from the universe at large. Nor can a man be separated from his ultimate good. He gave the impression that he had a Partner more real than his business associates and a faith in something more basic than can be seen and felt through the physical senses. This fact of the nearness of God caused me to conclude that if PL can so catch the imagination of a practical, trigger-minded and highly successful head of an international corporation, it must have practical value. If it can persuade a businessman that his life can be sensitized, his career heightened, and his happiness increased, this could be a major reason for this emerging religion getting a foothold in our Western world. For the question we pragmatic Americans are beginning to ask more and more of religion is simply this: Does it work in life?

Don Steele said that PL worked. It worked instantly, though it required dedicated effort. A man had to learn certain techniques and disciplines.

"The secret word with me," he was saying, "is *Makoto*. *M-a-k-o-t-o*. When you talk about Life-Is-Art, that's it. *Makoto*. I predict that the Western world will learn this word. What is *Makoto*? I call it a workable, practical life-style."

I had heard the word *Makoto* many times and had often run across it in the PL lexicon. Along with *Mishirase* and *Mioshie*, I had jotted it down in my mind as one of the "three ms," which made it easier for me to remember all three: *Mishirase, Mioshie, Makoto*—a way of thinking, a style of life.

Mishirase and *Mioshie* are indigenously PL, but *Makoto* has been part of Oriental religious terminology for a long time. PL is merely making it relevant and new and causing

45

it to become as familiar as the word *Kami*. I had a feeling that if we understood *Kami* a bit better, *Makoto* would become more clear. *Kami* has many meanings. It is used synonymously for deity, but that is only part of it. If you talk about a name for God, the word *Kami* alone will hardly suffice, though it is usually included in references to God. For example, Shinto is *Kami-n-michi*, which means the "Way-of-the-Gods." The reference to God in PL is Mioya-Ookami.

It has always been a belief among Japanese that true service to the *Kami* is by way of *Makoto*, an approach to life through a consciousness of our complete partnership with God. *Makoto* was used in Shinto to describe "the humble, single-minded reaction which wells up within us when we touch directly or indirectly upon the workings of the *Kami*, when we know that the *Kami* exist, and have the assurance of their close presence with us."

While on the one hand we sense our baseness and imperfection in the presence of God, we are also overwhelmed with joy and gratitude at our realization that it is possible to live within the harmony of the *Kami* nature. While the conditions of life surrounding us remain the same, *Makoto* inspires a new life-impression in us. When a person has *Makoto* then naturally there appears a conduct which is virtuous and reverent. To have someone say that his mind and life are "*Makoto*" was always considered an evidence of a high plane of living.

"*Makoto*," Don Steele was saying via the cassette, "means really believing that there is a material world and a spiritual world. And it is knowing that there is a bridge that brings these worlds together and makes us realize that both are ruled by the Almighty Power that made and governs the universe so flawlessly and with such split-second thoroughness that when we catch on to the timing of it everything is in our favor."

He once called it, "Our total synchronization with God."

"*Makoto*," the voice continued, "begins with the belief in the concept that the material world is here for us to make use of. These materials do not belong to us really, and I do not say this in the sense that we should not have property rights or personal possessions or the right to put our money in a bank or put a fence around our land to denote ownership, but what I mean is that the materials are here, have always been here all through history, and people who owned great fortunes really came into this world empty-handed. They did not bring material things with them into this life and, of course, after breathing their last mortal breath, they went out empty-handed. Therefore, in the eternal scheme of things, they really just had the use of their paints and their brushes and their canvases, and their banks and cattle ranches and their fortunes as they worked out the artistry of their lives.

"So we do live in a material world and the materials are here and we could never express ourselves without materials. We need materials, even if they provide nothing more than a place in which we sit and think, sheltered from the weather. Even a poet needs a pencil and paper to jot down his ideas. Materials are ours to use as long as we do not contribute destructively to mankind but quietly and constructively do our thing and make our contribution.

"Then when we fuse the material world with the spiritual world we have created a state of perfect liberty, and at that point we must deeply believe in *Mishirase* and *Mioshie*, and we come to truly understand *Makoto*.

"As an example, one day I was cut off short by a client of mine. He forced me to wait for three hours in my hotel room for a call that he had promised would come through immediately, and so on. Now at an earlier stage in my life I would have bitterly resented this man and this situation and I would have cut him off my list and become something of an enemy. I would have found pleasure in giving him a piece of my mind and reminding him that I don't have to take his gaff. But since I am now in PL and have learned a great deal about how the law of the universe works, I said to myself, 'How wonderful! I can hardly wait to see the next chapter and follow this chain of events to the end! There is more deep meaning in this than meets the eye!' "

Days later, Mr. Steele went to see this client in the expectation that the man was deliberately seeking to make it easier for them to sever their relationship, or trying to manipulate things so that Steele would withdraw from the whole thing under protest. Instead, it developed that this very situation had invisibly shielded Steele and his company from a questionable legal and ethical circumstance through which the client was passing.

"Even an appointment I later had," Don Steele reported, "which was again cancelled and which kept me from going to a distant city, was so timed by the Power that rules the universe that I was on hand when several important out-of-the-country clients came to town unexpectedly to see me. I then realized that everything had been put together and fit together because I took this *Mishirase* in stride.

"These raps on the knuckles that sting for a while *are Mishirase*, but the *Mioshie* is, as Jesus might have said, when we learn that, 'Not my will but Thine be done.' Looking at life this way is *Makoto*. It is believing that those raps on the knuckles, those minor accidents, those major accidents, those illnesses, those business appointments that you think have gone wrong, those seeming reversals, those things that hit us are not just accidental, they are for a purpose, either to block our pathway from impending disaster, danger or discomfort, or to teach us a meaningful lesson.

"The person who has *Makoto* believes that this Power helps him when he is living within the circumference of the Twenty-one Precepts, and when we are with deep *Makoto* we are bridging our lives with the other world and at the same time expressing ourselves in the fullness of

48

art and science with expertise and skill. As long as we are doing this and not hurting anyone in the process and as long as we make use of our prayers and our discipline, a calmness comes over us and a power surges into us, and the moment this power takes over, everything happens. We are definitely on the beam. Our thoughts are transmitted to pertinent people, people are inspired to think of us, things happen in a divine plan, movements begin, we progress, we look at someone and he turns and looks at us. We think of someone and the person calls us. Our presence is felt. The power of PL is so great that when generated with deep *Makoto* we are guided by the dynamic and love of universal law just as all nature is so guided and sustained.

"*Makoto* is a way of saying, 'God is! I am! I am art! I am self-expression! I am living in the interest of others as well as myself!'

"*Makoto* is turning the precepts of PL into affirmations and repeating them and repeating them until they are like burned threads to be woven into the fabric and tapestry of our lives.

"*Makoto* is such a big word that it is like a magic sceptre of some sort. When you have *Makoto* you have the strength of a Solomon, of a Shakespeare, of a Miki. You have the strength of people who stand on their two feet in this world, bowing only to God, respecting and giving their community and their government good citizens, good PL people. *Makoto* expresses itself in all community life, but it must begin within oneself. It must be believed in and trusted in and proved within oneself."

At this point I realized again how personal Don Steele's introduction to PL had actually been. He first heard about it in connection with public relations work in the Orient and this inspired him to read and reflect on the Twenty-one Precepts. There was nothing particularly revolutionary in them, but they were provocative and made him review his own religious odyssey. Once a Seventh Day Adventist,

49

a seeker in various other faiths and philosophies, he had accumulated a good deal of information and had heard religion discussed in both pulpit and marketplace. His conclusions, before he came into PL, were "like statements scribbled on scraps of paper and stuffed into a desk drawer." Often, in times of need, he pulled open this figurative drawer and selected a few of these scraps at random, trying to put them into operation.

Now it seemed to him as if the Twenty-one Precepts were taking the scribbled notes and organizing them in businesslike fashion. They were at least getting from the desk drawer onto the desk, and as he looked at them he felt that everything he needed and wanted had been compressed into these twenty-one succinct statements. There were no prohibitions in PL, only challenges. There were no "Thou shalt nots," only obvious declarations which were waiting to be tested and proved.

Don had been troubled for some time with a dermatological condition which a specialist had described as cancerous growths on his forehead. The sun had all but ruined his skin and the doctor said he wished he could give him a new face. It was decided that he should have plastic surgery but there was no guarantee that this would correct the basic cancerous condition.

At this time Don Steele had been only a few days in PL but he nonetheless put his situation into the hands of a PL minister, Rev. Koreaki Yano, who had recently come from Japan to serve as Chief Minister of North America. In discussing Don's situation, the story came up about the seeming miracle of a young man in the navy who had recovered from a major operation in a day and who had rejoined his buddies with such suddenness that even the M.D. called it an "astonishing recovery."

In a state of deep belief, Don asked Rev. Yano for prayers. The minister wrote on a slip of paper an affirmation that the plastic surgery would be a complete, unquestioned success and that the cancer situation would disappear.

It was after this that I met Don Steele and understood the enthusiasm with which he discussed this first adventure with PL. "I was a bloody mess," he said. "After an hour and a half in surgery, I wasn't surprised to hear that even the nurse had passed out. Furthermore, I had been given only Novocain because the doctor wanted me to have control over certain facial muscles. Yet the next morning it was as if an angel had smoothed things out, as if the hand of God had touched my face. The doctor could not believe it. Within three days all the stitches were removed and I was really a new man physically and spiritually."

He has had no more evidence of skin cancer and nearly two years have passed. He believed that his daily prayers and the prayers of PL ministers kept the threat in an arrested state. He candidly told me that he felt his straightforward approach of blending his physical body with God's universal care was the secret and that this "miracle" could have happened through any spiritual teaching if he could have reached this same unified state. PL was, for him, the answer because it represented the most direct distance between two points: the material and the ethereal world.

What was I to say? I who had heard of healing miracles and testimonies of changed lives all around the world in various faiths and disciplines? I could only agree. I wished it were possible to get one of the secrets of Don Steele and others like him across to all followers of various faiths, namely that these instances of the seemingly supernormal are normal, and that at the heart of them is the miracle of great expectations. When I mentioned this to Don he responded with a burst of enthusiasm.

"Great expectations!" he exclaimed. "That's really *Makoto!* When we get up in the morning we expect to see the sun. When we hear a robin we expect to see signs of spring. When we see the lightning we expect to hear the thunder. When we look at nature we expect to see it respond in its proper season, cherry blossoms or autumn foliage, falling snow or summer storms, all depend upon great expectations!

When we see people we expect to see them as they are. When we view the world we expect to see things go right. They should go right. They do go right. When they go wrong we are surprised. That is because we instinctively believe in the rightness of people, the world, and God.

"In God's divine plan He has written above it all, 'Have great expectations!' Man was put on earth to be a happy human being. Troubles and woe are brought on ourselves by failing to understand *Mishirase* and *Mioshie*. *Makoto* means looking at the adversities of life and at anything abnormal and asking, 'Why? Why has this happened? What have I done? What caused this? Is this a blessing in disguise? Have I lost my humility? Has success gone to my head? Have I lost my concern for the other fellow?'

"It takes only a few seconds to ask these things, and *Makoto* represents this asking. It is only by self-examination that a *Mioshie* can take place. Then, as if by a mystic magic we are lifted out of the bad situation and the healing process begins. And if we can keep this shaft of light shining into our consciousness, we have truly bridged our material lives with the spiritual world. This is the hard core, the nitty-gritty, the point at which the pilot knows he is in direct contact with the tower. And when we are on automatic pilot with the great Being that runs the show and we have this feeling of unfailing assurance during our flight through life, this is *Makoto!*"

To me it was all in divine order, though not without its amazing overtones. To think that even before I ever knew I would be going on this particular trip to Japan, long before I suspected that my journey, if it should take place, would be aboard the 747, before all of this, I recorded the voice and views of a man who used an illustration of the automatic pilot in our relationship with God and life. This went even beyond great expectations! This argued strongly for some over-belief in a wisdom and a planning higher and greater than our own. That I had brought the tape and the cassette with me, that all fit so perfectly into the scheme of things, this, too, was part of the divine timing.

Makoto. It was a word which once heard and once experienced would never permit a person to be quite the same again. How, I wondered, would it be interpreted by Japanese members of PL when I met them and talked with them at the Tondabayashi headquarters? I would be meeting Don and Evelyn Steele there, too, and other Americans who had been drawn by the tantalizing power of PL.

Chapter Four

"OYASHIKIRI"

WHEN THE LATE afternoon sun flung a shower of crimson against the windows of our plane, I felt that if I had my way about religious services I would insist they be held, at least occasionally, in the sky. It would not be a traditional church service with hymns, sermon and Sunday offering, but rather a time in which we would catch something of the nature of God and better sense His secret expression in each of us. For this a good text would be a reading from the third chapter of the PL manual:

> Man is God manifested as a human being. Man is not God Himself but man possesses the essential qualities of God.

These words would become more meaningful as we swept through space realizing that though we are earthlings we are also transcendent, and though we have our limitations there is something within us that is not bound by a four dimensional world. Altitude would give us a new spiritual attitude. PL says

> God embraces everything. Good and evil, beauty and ugliness, truth and falsehood, happiness and misfortune, everything is nestled in His bosom. God is power and love that, while embracing everything, creates everything, nurtures everything, and makes everything progress and develop. Everything, originating thus in God, always makes movement toward progress and development by trying to transform evil into truth, and misfortune into happiness.

I would ask our high altitude worshippers to think about the artistry of life and the wonderful magic of faith which are credentials of great religions everywhere. PL is no exception. Though some have called it a faith tailored to an industrial world, it has its deeply mystical meanings.

For example, there is *Oyashikiri* which, according to definition, is "a petition to God for the full benefits of the Universal Power." *Oyashikiri* is literally the "breath or spirit of God" and to those who do not like the word "mystical" it simply means that they believe this breath or spirit to be a normal, functional aspect of life, which it surely is. At any rate, *Oyashikiri* is a prayer and a ritual in which the spiritual presence of the Patriarch is united with that of his people, creating a pool of supranormal power.

Oyashikiri takes us into the heart of the PL movement. As a ritual it is as universal as is the Mass in Catholicism. As an act of worship it has an impact comparable to the devotion of the Islamic people when they bow toward their holy city of Mecca, Hijaz. As a revelation it is as sacred as the Jewish torah, as a symbol it is as cherished as the mandala is in Buddhism, as a prayer it is as important as "Our Father" is to the Christian. As a mystery it is as much a part of gracious living as the pause before the *tokonoma* in any Oriental home. But having said this we still have not caught the real meaning of *Oyashikiri*.

It involves a highly corporate experience. In *Oyashikiri* you are not only awakening power within yourself, but receiving it through the psychic force of the founders and developers of the PL faith: Kanada, Tokuharu Miki, and the Patriarch. These principles PL devotees devoutly believe, and if outsiders do not believe them I can only say that in PL as in all religions only those know the power who live the life. To fully understand PL, you must be PL.

Oyashikiri represents the heart of meditation, prayer, ceremonial, and reflective communication between God and self. In all of these the PL devotee knows at his deepest feeling level that the Patriarch, Oshieoya-sama, takes the obligation of every true prayer upon himself. In fact, he has told his people that he assumes full responsibility for doing what he believes is the absolute will of God for his followers. He takes an oath to this effect. It is a potent part of PL teaching that if you believe this oath and trust in it, your prayer will be heard and answered. If, however, you insist on getting the blessings of Oyashikiri without following the Twenty-one Precepts you are "fishing without bait."

It is unrealistic and an indication of greediness to want the blessings of God without the intention of obeying God. As Oshieoya has taken an oath, so it is expected that PL members will also take an oath to be true to the teachings of the Twenty-one Precepts, one of which clearly states that, "All things exist in mutual relationship to one another."

This is a profound teaching, as are all the precepts when we get into their philosophical meaning. Mutual relationship means the function of the one-whole-integrated-universe which is the work of *Kami* (Spirit). It stresses the fact that everything that exists has its own purpose, capability and limit and that the relationship between these "existences" is a function of the will which can create new dynamics of expression as it projects its image out of the

57

integrated body. Or it can gain new creative understanding as it explores more deeply *into* the integrated body. Both "adventures," according to PL, are dependent upon the decision of the will and both will prove the mutual relationship existing between all things.

The hub of this mutuality is *Oyashikiri*, which we have referred to as the "breath or spirit of God." *Oyashikiri* is made graphic in the PL symbol, the *Omitama*, found in the home of every true PL member. It looks like this:

a golden, wheel-like emblem consisting of twenty-one rays emanating from a central hub, a mirror symbolic of the sun.

■ 2 ■

Ask a PL member about the meaning of *Oyashikiri* as it is used in meditation and you will get a different answer from that found in such religions as Zen, Hinduism or mystical Christianity. There are no prolonged moments of solemn seeking for *sazen* or *samadhi* or beatific visions. There is in PL no agonized search for the "presence of God."

"PL," we will be told, "is interested in the present, everyday, workaday world. Religion is life, and life is living. We are not concerned about the kind of meditation that makes a person a hermit or that sends people into caves or cells trying to find God. We have no type of meditation that makes a person 'unconscious.' We are interested in becoming consciously alive and alert. We prepare ourselves for the tasks and assignments of each day in offices, in our homes, wherever we are, and if we are a hundred percent involved in what we are doing, we may call this the PL' way of meditation or concentration."

Not that PL people are devoid of a sense of wonder when they are alone or that they are not aware of the cosmic rhythm of nature. The Patriarch once said that he felt deep meditation when he went fishing, and it may be that this was also part of his symbolism when he suggested one should not "fish without bait," but, rather, have God and goodness in mind at all times. But the point is that PL meditation is more like concentration and personal reflection than it is a search for a particularized, transcendental experience.

Whenever I asked the obvious Christian question, "When do PL people have their 'quiet time?'" the answer was something like this:

"Most of us begin our days in front of the symbol of prayer, the *Omitama*. We face it, either standing or sitting, and making our *Oyashikiri*. This is our meditation and we concentrate on what we hope to accomplish for the day. Usually the husband and wife or the entire family spend a few moments in this way. We ask the blessing of God and the direction of God in our activities. In the good sense of the word, our prayer is a desire to do well whatever we are called upon to do. We also listen to guidance or hunches or intuition which are ways that God may speak to us."

Without these prayers, without *Oyashikiri*, PL people have a feeling they would begin the day devoid of God's presence. This would not be practical, and PL is a practical religion. Answers to prayer are not always expected to be precise or in keeping with the person's request. Prayer is a method of finding guidelines and direction, in getting at the heart of *Mioshie* and discovering God's will. Actually PL is close to the Christian concept of "not my will but Thine." Hence the belief in hunches, in telltale signs, in guidance.

Often when things do *not* work out as prayer-planned, the PL follower has learned to say, "Well, that is very wonderful. God has something even better in mind."

"I wanted to be an international diplomat," one member told me. "I prayed and studied toward this goal. I passed the examinations but while at Tokyo University, I became very much interested in PL. My oldest brother was a minister in the field and I also was led to become a PL minister. Many of my friends at the university thought I was making a mistake because they felt I was well qualified for a diplomat, but it was right. It was God's guidance. My oldest brother understood because he knew Oshieoya-sama, the Patriarch, and he had a similar experience of being guided.

"He once broke both legs in a ski run. In the war his commander had asked the men which one would volunteer to make the ski run and my brother eagerly stepped forward. He was the only one who volunteered and in racing down the dangerous slope, he broke his legs. When he asked the Patriarch for the divine instruction of *Mioshie* as to why he broke his legs, the Patriarch said, 'Do not volunteer too eagerly unless it is a command or order.' Years later when my brother was on shipboard, he received a telegram from naval headquarters which said, 'Leave ship at the next port, you have been appointed to be an instructor of navy school.' He said to himself that here he had just fulfilled a lifetime dream to be on shipboard and now he was ordered off. He thought this was very unfair because he did not want to be an instructor; he wanted to be a sailor. But he remembered the Patriarch's words which had told him he should obey a command or an order. So he did. He left the ship. Well, that ship was sunk several days later with much loss of life. My brother went on into his new career, then finally into the PL ministry, knowing and believing in God's guidance and in the Patriarch's divine instructions. How could he do otherwise?"

It is this kind of trust, this belief that prompts every PL believer to approach the *Omitama* by himself or with his wife and family. After their prayers, they frequently discuss the affairs of the day, analyzing and correcting each other's conduct and actions, fitting together the pieces of God's plan as they see it. The *Omitama* is, in a way, the silent counselor in a kind of sensitivity session, and among religious groups that I have known it would be difficult to find one in which members respond more understandingly to suggestion or advice, even if it hurts, just as long as it leads to a more artistic, trustful life.

"We have perfect liberty in talking together about our actions," a husband and wife told me, "because we know we are talking in the presence of God. This, to us, is meditation. This is part of *Oyashikiri.*"

■ 3 ■

Christianity has nothing quite like the *Omitama* or *Oyashikiri*. Certainly in Protestantism we have no particular emblem or symbol, not even an altar, and rarely a religious picture. We have no sacred enshrinement such as that suggested by the *Omitama* to which visitors automatically and courteously pay respect when they come into a PL oriented home. The Christian cross, perhaps our most revered symbol and sign, suggests an event and a Person and an act of God. The *Omitama* points to no Saviour, no suffering, no specific historic happening, no theological plan, not even to a special act of God. Yet, in the *Omitama*, PL people see the totality of the Twenty-one Precepts and when they say the single word, *Oyashikiri*, even without any other prayer, they feel the power.

We have no equivalent of this kind with which to invoke God's power, granted that we have many expressions with which to pray. The closest Christian approximation of *Oyashikiri* would be "God is with me," or "God be with me" and we would conceivably repeat these phrases in time of both worship and need. *Oyashikiri* is different. The prefix "*Oya*" appears frequently in the Shinto faith under the meaning of "God the Parent" or "the Parenthood of God." *Oyashikiri* is interpreted by religious scholars as "the accomplished resolve of the Parent," and PL, as we have seen, defines it as the way by which the merit and help of *Oshie-oya* is made available to the true believer.

One of the earliest testimonials during my PL research was that of a young father who told me, "My son was struck by a car. I got the report while I was at work. Because it was impossible for me to get away immediately, I did *Oyashikiri*. It was as if I actually felt the help that came to my son. Something told me everything would be all right. I worked more calmly and as soon as I could get away, I went to my boy's side at the hospital. He *was* all right. The doctor said it was miraculous that he was injured only so little considering the violence of the accident."

Another testimonial in my notes was that of a young PL member who ran out of gas on a Los Angeles freeway. Anyone who has experienced this knows how welcome the proper prayer or a miracle would be! Repeating "*Oyashikiri*" kept this young man calm and, according to his testimony, brought him unusually quick assistance from a car that was prompted to stop.

My own adventure in a similar situation was even more dramatic. I was on the freeway late one night when I noticed that my gas gauge registered far below the empty mark. I turned off the nearest ramp in what I knew was one of the tougher sections of town, but I was sure there would be service stations nearby. There usually are. But after I had passed two that were closed (it being midnight), the car began to sputter and I was forced to coax it to the curb. I locked it and began to walk.

The poorly lighted street was deserted but for a single passerby, a hatless man with his coat collar turned up, walking slowly. He was like a silhouette, a shadow, a man in his thirties. I asked him how far it was to a station. Sullenly he said, "Four blocks," and then offered to walk with me if I was afraid. I felt less afraid alone and told him I could manage. He shrugged and turned away.

For some reason, in a rueful kind of gamemanship, I caught myself saying, "*Oyashikiri, Oyashikiri, Oyashikiri*" as I walked with quick steps in the direction the stranger had pointed out. A reassuring Mobil sign shimmered far ahead. Whenever I passed anyone, a couple, a drunk, several slow moving cars, I said, "*Oyashikiri, Oyashikiri!*"

I got a can of gas, three gallons. The night man who was alone said I was stupid to be out on the street and I think he was even scared of me when I came walking in at that hour. I paid him, left a deposit for the container, and started back to the car, all the time saying, "*Oyashikiri, Oyashikiri!* and visualizing the *Omitama* emblem as I remembered it. Not only did I need protection for myself, I was also thinking of the car left at the curb.

A police car cruised the street. As it slowed down, I raised my hand, hoping the cops would give me a lift. All they did was flash a light on me and pass me by. When I got within about a block and a half of my car, there stood the man who had given me the directions and whose help I had turned down. He was puffing at a cigarette. I kept approaching with my mental, "*Oyashikiri, Oyashikiri!*"

I was about to pass him when he fell in step with me. "I see you made it," he mumbled.

He suggested that the gas can must be heavy. I told him it wasn't too bad. "Well," he said, "let me take it." So saying he jerked it from my hand and carried it to the car. He stuck the nozzle of the container into the tank and began pouring in the gas. My "*Oyashikiri*" was getting more serious now and when he got through and put the gas cap back on, I took two quarters from my pocket and said, "Thank you for helping me. That was very kind of you."

He picked up the cigarette stub he had laid on the curb, then pulled open the car door and tossed the empty container inside.

"I don't want that money," he said. And he stood there looking at me. Just looking. Trying to figure me out. I did not know what to say. He really looked sad and a bit confused. "Is something wrong?" I asked.

He threw away his cigarette. "Yes, there is," he said, and stuffed his hands in his coat pockets. "I had a fight with my wife tonight," he said, "and I left the house. I've been walking the damn street wondering if I should go back."

I put my hand on his arm. I don't know why. I just wanted to touch him. "Go back," I found myself saying. "Please go back to her. Everything will be all right."

He looked at me as if no one had ever talked to him like that and after a moment, he said, "Maybe I will, fellow, maybe I will." And he walked away.

■ 3 ■

What, I wondered, would I learn about *Oyashikiri* at the PL headquarters? I had been told that some exciting experiments were taking place in the use of *Oyashikiri* prayers over plants and that highly scientific work was being done in the field of spiritual healing. I had been advised that it would be an unforgettable sight to see several thousand *hoshiin* (devoted worshippers) do the *Oyashikiri* ritual together at the great service, especially on the Patriarch's birthday when the colorful festival *Kyoshu-Tanjosai* would be held.

I was prepared, if the occasion required, to pray before the PL emblem as I had prayed in many Japanese temples and shrines before, gracious prayers and prayer forms as one finds them everywhere in the new religions of Japan.

What was more, I had attended an *Omitama* enshrinement ceremony in a home in Los Angeles. The young couple, parents of two children, had recently come into the PL fellowship and were having their *Omitama* consecrated. It was an impressive event with family and guests gathered in front of the fireplace mantel where the *Omitama* had earlier been placed under its protective glass dome. In this case the *Omitama* emblem was on a golden stem some twelve inches high. The reverence pervading the entire ceremony, the prayers and obeisance, were reminiscent of any altar service in which the object of corporate worship is enshrined. This *Omitama* had been blessed by the Patriarch, and the PL minister who approached it was in full ceremonial attire. A deep blue robe, offset by a pure white shoulder cassock, a white ritual cap, and white gloves, added charm to his artistic movements.

Body erect, proudly sincere, the young minister advanced to within arm's length of the *Omitama* where he paused to fix his eyes upon it as in a moment of personal identification. Evidently in this symbol he saw and felt the presence not only of *Oshieoya* and the teaching of PL but also the power of the PL deity, *Mioya-Ookami*. Gloved hands at his side, he now placed them with finger tips touching the knees, bowed low, then stood fully upright as if in his straight bearing he gave evidence of deep affinity with the *Omitama*.

Hands at side once more, there followed immediately the ritual position in which the fingers of the two hands are intertwined, tips of thumbs and forefingers touching to form a circle, a symbol of the sun, while the hands are held somewhat below the solar plexus. Then, palms just barely touching, the hands are raised forehead high and the sun symbol is repeated with fingers outstretched like rays of light.

This done, the palms are once more brought together and lowered to a conventional prayer position over the chest. With head bowed, in a posture familiar to religions everywhere, the minister made his silent prayer. This is the moment of deep *Makoto* when *Oyashikiri* is mentally repeated or a special prayer is said, after which the hands are again lowered and returned to the sides of the body. Another low bow, again an intertwining sun symbol as at the start of the ritual, a slight nod of gratitude to the *Omitama*, and the worshipper retreats reflectively with folded hands.

Dramatically the minister unrolled a parchment and read the enshrinement invocation: "Before the new and sacred altar to the noble and merciful God, we reverently pray and say: Today is the most joyous day among joyous days, most significant among significant days, which enables us to have the Enshrinement Ceremony of *Koy-Omitama*, symbol of prayer, reverently welcoming to this home of Mr. and Mrs. Coley Knight, the God *Mioya-Ookami* and the spirits of their ancestors.

"From this time forth, may You protect and guard this house and its family, as they take a vow in Your presence to live and follow the way of man all the time, day and night; the way of man which they learn through the teachings of PL.

"Let them have infinite Glory of *Oyashikiri* with growing prosperity to this house and the family of Knight for this generation and forthcoming generations.

"May God behold and bless them, for they will faithfully follow the teaching of PL as long as they live; live an artistic life for the sake of men and society by devotion to other people through the grace of *Oyashikiri*."

Then the vows were taken and *Oyashikiri* was prayed by the hosts and special friends and members of PL. Following this, the PL prayer, used at all services, was intoned in Japanese. It is in the form of a four or five minute chant and begins, "*Takahikari Masu Mioya-Ookami Way. . . .*" Following it in translation, I learned that it said, "Noble and merciful God, *Mioya-Ookami*, Thou hast created all things and dost make all things ceaselessly in accord with Thy Divine Plan, in harmony with Thy Plan, and by Thy grace all mankind who are brought to birth in accord with Thy Creation are endowed with individuality and intelligence to live an artistic life." It speaks of *Mishirase* and *Mioshie* and embraces a plea for strength to "express my true and sincere individuality in a life of art."

The mystical power of PL had now been established in the home. The link between the devotees and *Oshieoyasama* had been sealed. And as I stood among the worshipers and felt their security of faith, I thought again how the concept of God is everywhere personified in man's will to believe.

Surely this is the secret of *Oyashikiri*. The inner world of the spiritual life grows in ratio to man's believability and trust in the makers and founders of his faith. It is not through searching or feverish groping that we find God by whatever name we call Him, it is by our awareness of His Spirit coming to life in us.

You will-to-believe that there is power in your prayer, that the method that has been taught you by a master teacher is correct, and you put it to a test in the firm belief that it will work whether you are in a 747 or in a quiet home before the *Omitama*. It has long been a theory of mine, and PL confirms it, that there must first be a wish or a need to believe, then a will, and then the experiment or adventure which makes the wish and the will come true.

We have tried all too long to reverse the process. We have had a tendency to say, "If I *knew* this were true I would act upon it." And we have refused to act. PL says, "Act upon it and prove its truth for yourself."

This, in fact, is the challenge with which this new religion confronts the institutionalized churches. I once said, "Religion cannot prove its full potential until it has been tried, but there is a reluctance to try it until it has proved its full potential." PL has solved this dilemma by persuading its people to try the PL approach and prove it for themselves. This is where we all stand in the eternal quest. Whether it is *Oyashikiri* or *Our Father* or *Om* or whatever the word or symbol or the reality may be, until we step out on faith and

67

make our prayers in a spirit of unquestioned faith, nothing is going to happen to change our life or change the world.

Through all these thoughts, the 747, like the art of life, moved toward its destination, carrying along the Song of Self. Many PL members feel this way about their devotions in front of the *Omitama*. Though they travel throughout the world, they never really leave their place of meditation, their real identity. It is here, in these moments, in these remembrances and repetitions of *Oyashikiri* spoken aloud or silently with a believing heart that the power of PL is realized and released.

There is a Japanese saying, "If you look for the source of the River Yoshino you will find it in the drops of water beneath the moss and in the drops of dew that fall from the reeds." So it is with the moments of prayer. When we are roused into believing in our own unique artistry of life, in that moment religion becomes a living force.

And that is why PL people at work and at play, on dark city streets or worshipping before the *Omitama*, have their moments when they pray, "*Oyashikiri, Oyashikiri!*"

"Paradise," said the Patriarch, "is waiting in every true believer's soul."

Chapter Five

THE
PEOPLE

■ 1 ■

THE LARGEST plane in the world came down in the largest city in the world at 9:30 P.M. in a drizzling rain. It taxied to a stop a quarter of a mile from the terminal and stood there dominating the scene of blinking lights and interweaving vehicles, impatiently waiting the giant ramp being hauled into place.

We were escorted under umbrellas down the long flight of steps to the transportation buses, then whisked away to customs and the usual formalities. From here on I was under the expert care and guidance of Rev. Koreaki Yano and also three young men who had come to International Airport from a PL church in Tokyo. Their assignment was to facilitate matters at customs and then accompany Rev. Yano and me to a waiting plane headed for Osaka.

It was split-second scheduling, for our clipper ship had been slowed by headwinds and we had lost time because of the rain drenched landing, but there was evidently nothing quite like the intuitive timing among PL people when involved in PL plans. This fact was to be impressed upon me continually during my Japanese stay, and it began here with our dash with baggage to the jam-packed JAL plane which was actually being held for us, a most unusual courtesy. We waved our *sayonaras* to the Tokyo delegates and hurried aboard.

The plane, so crowded that Rev. Yano and I could not sit together, gave me just the chance I needed to do some last minute homework, a quick refresher on the PL glossary and certain details which now, since I was nearing location, became more relevant.

SEICHI: general designation for the PL headquarters.
TONDABAYASHI: the town where the Seichi is located, a city of some fifty thousand.
HABIKINO: name for the overall twenty-five hundred acres which comprise the PL compound.
PL KYODAN: the PL denomination.
GOSEIDEN: the great temple at Habikino.
RENSEI: Prominent PL youth training program.
KYOSHU-TANJOSAI: the Patriarch's birthday festival, April 8.
KYOSOSAI: anniversary of the death of the First Patriarch, August 1.
SHINKYO: spiritual state of mind.
TENJINGOITSU: awareness of the harmony of God and man.

The list was long and tantalizing. It included the three "M's": *Mishirase, Mioshie* and Makoto. It urged me to reflect once more on the meaning of *Oyashikiri*, on the Patriarch who was called Oshieoya or Oshieoya-sama and on Tsugioya, title for the successor-designate to the Patriarch. I also reviewed the life of Tokumitsu Kanada, who influenced Tokuharu Miki, the First Patriarch (Kyoso), and recalled the unfoldment of the faith from the time it was called *Hito-no-Michi* (1931) into what is now PL.

Then there were the Twenty-one Precepts which I was determined to commit to memory, and not to memory only but to heart:

1. Life is art.
2. Man's life is a succession of self-expressions.
3. Man is a manifestation of God.
4. Man suffers if he fails to express himself.
5. Man loses his true self when swayed by feelings and emotions.
6. Man's true self is revealed when his ego is effaced.
7. All things exist in mutual relationship to one another.
8. Live radiantly as the "sun."
9. All men are equal.
10. Strive for creating mutual happiness.
11. Have true faith in God.
12. There is a way (function) peculiar to every "name" (existence).
13. There is a way for men, and there is another way for women.
14. All is for world peace.
15. All is a mirror.
16. All things progress and develop.
17. Comprehend what is most essential.
18. At every moment man stands at the crossroads of good and evil.
19. Act when your intuition dictates.
20. Live in perfect unity of mind and matter.
21. Live in Perfect Liberty.

I looked across to Koreaki Yano sitting two rows away in our Osaka plane engrossed in a copy of *Geitjutsu Seikatsu*. This magazine, published under the direction of Patriarch Miki, was recognized as one of the best fine-art journals in the Orient, and I could well see why. Its amazing photography, calligraphy, beauty in format and subtlety of color surpassed anything we had in the Western world.

Rev. Yano, a slightly built, short, mild-mannered man, was an able poet in his own right. Sensitive, an able interpreter of PL doctrine, he was building a reputation for himself as

PL's Chief Minister of North America. I had been with him on several occasions in his Glendale church and had been impressed, as were his parishioners, with his quiet dedication to every detail of his ministry. In conversations with him, I soon discovered that he was thoroughly original in his thinking and that his most exciting quality lay in his firm and gracious talent for leadership.

His father, the Reverend Jiro Yano, whom I looked forward to meeting at Seichi, was administrative head of the educational work at PL headquarters and an influential leader in the PL *Kyodan*. Don Steele and his wife, Evie, close friends of the Yanos, would also be on hand at Habikino to share in the Patriarch's birthday observance. Thousands of devoted PL members (*hoshiin*) would be there, together with spiritual assistants (*hoyoshi*) and devoted pilgrims (*Kaigai-Dansan*) from many parts of the world. I got to wondering whether, when Koreaki Yano's leadership effected the expansion of PL across America, we of the Western world would be turned off or on by the Japanese vocabulary so descriptive in this new and persuasive faith, one which more and more seemed to contain a new approach to the psychology of religion of our time. Just what this psychology actually was, I would have to see.

■ 2 ■

At the Osaka airport another trio of young PL devotees was waiting to welcome us. Only one spoke English but he and Rev. Yano served as excellent interpreters. In no time at all we were acquainted and settled in the limousine where the white-gloved chauffeur had been complacently waiting. Again I had the feeling that behind the easy-going "life-is-art attitude" of this delegation, an almost computerized functioning of details was in operation, issuing straight out of the official offices at Seichi, a short hour's drive away.

It was now nearly midnight; a raw, damp, rainy midnight

with the traffic of industrial Osaka surprisingly heavy. Streets were under construction and it could have been a trying trip but for the high enthusiasm and outright joy of our carful of PL people. "How was your trip? How was the 747? Are you comfortable?" There were answers to my many questions about Seichi and its activities, but never any attempt to over-sell the PL movement or any hint of "wait till you see. . . ." this or that. It is one of the subtleties of Japanese life to leave a great deal to the imagination. I had, of course, seen pictures of the PL grounds and knew what to expect—the incredibly large school buildings with their circular dormitories, the equally monumental assembly halls, the retreat centers, art and cultural buildings, the modern hospital and medical research center.

All this I now looked forward to, but as far as the philosophy of PL was concerned, this began to reflect itself immediately in these Japanese PL members, in their conversation and their personalities. They were a happy people and basic in their attitude was a fundamental concept: "You yourself become happy as the result of making others happy." Usually people think of making themselves happy, but in PL the idea is to make others happy first. If you try to satisfy others according to your own idea of happiness you may even make them unhappy! To put it in a Japanese-ism which made the idea even more forceful, it went like this, "Don't think of your side. If you live to your own side, that is ego. If you live to others' benefit, that is Truth. Present life is rather low in level because most people do only what is profitable to their egos. PL changes all that."

So we talked, and the miles ticked by through sloshing highways and incessant traffic until one of the young men in the front seat tried out his English to tell me we were nearing our destination. "If we are lucky," he said, "maybe we will see Daiheiwato."

"Daiheiwato?" I asked, running my PL vocabulary hopefully through my mind.

"The Peace Tower," explained Rev. Yano.

Of course. I had seen pictures of this newly constructed giant memorial in Yano's church and had watched movies taken during its early stages when the steel girders were being welded at what seemed mile-high points in the sky. Daiheiwato, the Patriarch's original design of a memorial with a message: enough people have suffered and died in wars since time began; let us now live in harmony with God's love and law. The aim and end of Perfect Liberty is Perfect Peace.

It was then that suddenly through the curtain of rain, the incredible outline of the Peace Tower loomed over the Seichi grounds. Rev. Yano said, as if to himself, "Yes, there it is."

Our glimpse of it was brief and rain obscured. It was a grey-white pinnacle materializing out of the misty earth. I remembered the height, 550 feet, for I had associated it with the Washington Monument which it matches, lacking five feet, and with the Statue of Liberty which it tops by two hundred feet and more. It was a giant keeping watch over the PL *Kyodan*. Its gnarled base suggested struggle, its fingered tip stretching to the heavens pointed to God. This was Daiheiwato, my first veiled sight of it. And here was Seichi, not within Tondabayashi really, but a village of its own, free, with wide streets and the silhouetted outline of huge buildings, circular schools, and in the distance a columned jewel of white, the Goseiden on a hill.

The spaciousness of the grounds made distance deceptive and we continued to drive, winding our way past the outline of a lake and on to a four-story structure brilliantly lighted, the Palace. Midnight is an awkward time to arrive at one's destination, especially after thirteen hours on a plane, but when our chauffeur had us high and dry under the stone canopy in the circular driveway, when he opened the door for us in front of the sparkling glass foyer, it was as if the entire trip from Los Angeles to Habikino had been supernormally timed.

Six teenage girls, spotless in white blouses and blue skirts, bowed low in their places on each side of the spacious carpeted entrance hall. A gracious hostess greeted us with a bow that surpassed any word of welcome she might have had. Four faultlessly trained young guards stood at salute while several staff members waited at the entrance to a luxurious reception room. The welcome was typically Japanese, plus PL's deep-grained yet thoroughly relaxed reminder that "Life Is Art."

If a Japanese greeting, as someone once said, is designed to make every visitor feel he is a V.I.P., my welcome at the Palace bore this out. When Rev. Yano ushered me into the expansive, deeply-carpeted reception room, a high-ceilinged, elegant place, I was intrigued by the fact that just off-center in the room was a large aquarium with fish so dazzlingly blue, fish so golden, fish so luminously rainbow-striped, so incredible in beauty that it was as though the out-of-doors had been brought in to give an astonishing Zen touch to the surroundings.

Fish are art. The piece of impressionistic sculpture rising from a pedestal farther on in the room was art. A genuine Picasso painting, the rhythm of calm and loveliness, all was pure art. Very well, *life* is art. But when you are absorbed by a beauty that gives refreshment to the soul after a long flight between continents, you must also conclude that art is life.

I was now escorted into a smaller but equally beautiful room, one of the special "offices" of Oshieoya. The atmosphere here was pure serenity, as if Patriarch Miki had put some of his well known words into demonstration: "Money and material exist as matter to express your true self, otherwise money and material themselves are no worth at all." Consequently, there was another Picasso here and a scroll bearing an Oshieoya ideogram. There were also an orchid arrangement and a bonzai tree.

As we seated ourselves in the comfortable chairs surrounding the highly polished "tea table," the teenage girls magically appeared at just the right moment with the traditional *o-cha* and refreshments in hand. Again it was all perfectly synchronized, this time as if on cue to the appearance of Tsugioya and his charming wife. Rev. Yano explained that this successor-designate to the Patriarch had been visiting nearby and, hearing that I had arrived, decided to drop in and add his greetings.

I was honored by this special courtesy from Tsugioya, the Rev. Tokuhito Miki. He is a busy man and held in great esteem by the people. A favorite with young people, he is much interested in sports, books, and the arts and is an active Rotarian. A man of medium height, made to appear more mature than his thirty years by virtue of a short cropped beard, this nephew of Oshieoya was well chosen by Patriarch Miki for the future leadership of PL, and I was to learn that there were those who already felt he had deeply mystical spiritual qualifications. Currently Tsugioya was learning English and knew more of it than I did Japanese, but no matter, there is a wordless language everyone speaks when surrounded by tranquility and friends.

Actually, during the days of my stay, this was the persistent basis for my evaluation of PL, the sense of inner communication of its people and their irresistible spiritual vitality. What better appraisal of religion's influence can we find? How else shall we judge faith's outreach or effectiveness than to sense what it does in and through the lives of its followers? What is the real test if not this transforming, transcendental spirit?

At least, just now at the close of a day that was actually two days in one, time-wise, it did not seem absurd to me that life is a succession of self-expressions, that courtesy and gentility do make us nobler manifestations of God, as the precepts say. Or perhaps it all came back to the Song of Self. Whatever it was, it was a precious feeling. It was good to be at Seichi. It was *Makoto.*

76

Early the following morning I heard singing. Chanting.
A kind of marching song that I listened to for a moment in
the luxury of my Western-style Palace room. I drew back
the heavily lined silken draperies on the huge picture frame
windows.

It was a grey and hazy dawning over Habikino but on the
Oriental wooden bridges that spanned the lake and led out
from the five-story dormitory or "retreat center," rows
upon rows of white clad young people were energetically
jogging to the open grounds, singing on their way. These
were the "*Rensei* youth" of the PL spiritual training program. *Rensei:* heart of the total work of PL Kyodan as far
as human engineering is concerned, and who would dis-
agree when they saw these countless hundreds winding
through the grounds? These delegates were predominantly
from Japan with a goodly representation from Brazil where
PL was currently flourishing. *Rensei:* four days of indoctrination, fun, fellowship, and the interesting paradox of
regimentation and "Perfect Liberty." To make the *Rensei*
pilgrimage is as important to PL members as a trip to the
Holy Land is for the Christian.

As these phalanxes fanned out across the compound on
their way to the training centers, I caught the dramatic sight
of them against the Peace Tower, looming in the distance.
Daiheiwato silent in its vigil. The *Rensei* youth dynamic in
their lust of life. Seichi, the "Eternal Spiritual Home" of
PL, envisioned by Tokuharu Miki when this territory was
wasteland, and developed by Oshieoya after false imprisonment, persecution and his father's death.

It was more than I had hoped for, to have this scene unfold before me through the windows of my room. The

grounds, of course, were thrilling enough with the marble temple and its golden *Omitama* just above the portico, the distant greenhouses, the wide asphalt streets decorated with huge paper lanterns, oceans of cherry trees ready to burst into bloom with the first touch of the sun, the lake almost at my feet and white swans swimming. There was also a large sculptured piece, "The Golden Tower of Life," as it was called, the work of Japan's famed Sofu Teshigawara. This was set in the "Garden of Poetry," so named because a large stone bore words written by Patriarch Miki, "My heart will rejoice when the green hills will come to pass." This was inscribed years ago when the hills were arid and brown and recalled the prophesy of Miki's father who had said, "The permanent headquarters must have green hills and abundant water."

And now the people.

"My parents had always told me about *Rensei*," a young man confided to me in mid-morning. "Ever since I was a little boy they used to say, 'Wait till you have visited Seichi. Wait till you have been with other young people at *Rensei*. Wait till you see what life is like in the beautiful center of PL.' I could hardly wait. It was like the fulfillment of a dream when I finally came.

"Here were hundreds of young people, boys and girls looking forward as I was to what would happen. When I got up on that first morning, very early, our instructor told us to make our beds. This was a new experience for me and I said to myself, 'Well, is this what my parents meant? This is not going to be any pleasure. Is *Rensei* all work and study and making beds?' Then the instructor told us to make our beds *artistically*. 'Make them as neat and perfect as you can,' he said. 'Life Is Art.' You see, everything we do should be done with art.

"That was a new one for me. To be challenged to make a bed artistically caught my imagination. I began to look within myself for new abilities and I remember how proud

I was of the way I made that bed, but not really proud either because everyone had done as well as I. Nor was there any competition really; each of us just tried to find the best expression within us that we could find. That was the way it was when we left the dormitory. We sang as we went to our classes. We jogged along together chanting and singing. There can be art in everything you do."

So he began to have a new outlook, a new overview on things, the molding of a new life-style. Whether it was making a bed or making a life, the idea was to express one's best in the doing of it. "Art," said Oshieoya "is the ability to enjoy whatever we do in a pleasant mood."

The instructors in the *Rensei* program are staff members of PL University and PL ministers, and there is also exposure to outside lecturers who have PL affiliation. Dormitory facilities accommodating more than a thousand *Rensei* students are available, and judging from the construction projects going on this number will be doubled and tripled in the immediate years ahead.

Rensei is the human nerve center of PL and when the young man quoted above confided to me that, "*Rensei* changed my life and I came away feeling that my parents had understated the wonder of these four days," he was echoing the reaction of the vast majority who suddenly find ordinary, commonplace, trivial assignments transformed into opportunities for artistic expression. The influence of this on PL young people is so obvious, yet so subtle, that it is as important and cohesive a factor in PL's growth as *Oyashikiri* itself, the prayer which, by the way, binds the heart and soul of *Rensei* students in the undeviating goal of the "good life."

There must be some among the thousands who have taken *Rensei* training through the years who may have negative views about the program, but I could find no one who had any comment but praise. Not only young students but adults, too, come to Seichi for this self-enshrinement period.

They begin their day with worship and prayer, listen to lectures, put in hours of manual labor, join in physical exercises, enjoy play-time, talent-time, talk-time, live cooperatively, study PL teachings, and close the four day session with a dramatic torchlight march to the tomb of Tokuharu Miki.

Sometime during their training they pause as I did one afternoon at the foot of marble stairs leading to the *sakaki* tree, which this same Tokuharu Miki had planted as a seedling and before which he performed worship in keeping with the request of his master, Kanada. Here at this sacred spot, loyal PL followers have inscribed their names on small stones and made a contribution to the upkeep of this honored shrine. I was convinced that many of those who came here feeling the need for instruction were really in need of love and found it in *Rensei*. They were also in need of inspiration and the discipline of *Rensei* and the tree of Kyoso helped in their discovery.

Historians have tended to gloss over the details of this phase of Tokuharu's life, his years of worship often in the face of ridicule and loneliness, but here at the site of the tree the story is spelled out and written in a legend for all to see.

"After I am gone," Kanada told Tokuharu Miki, "plant a *sakaki* tree at the place of my death and promise me that you will worship at it daily. One day a great and good man will appear who will carry forward the work we have begun. You will know him and recognize him and he will add three revelations to the eighteen teachings we already have."

The year was 1919 and at Kanada's passing, Tokuharu Miki did as he was told. The *sakaki* (*himorogi*) tree had always been revered in Shinto, but the seedling that Tokuharu planted was worshiped daily and uninterruptedly for five long years. In 1924 the "great and good man" prophesied by Kanada appeared, and not unexpectedly it was Tokuharu Miki himself. Refined by worship, heightened by meditation and spiritually matured, he experienced enlightenment and pronounced the three revelations foretold by his former teacher.

As I stood with several young people in *Rensei* training, I told them our American story of the Great Stone Face in which Nathaniel Hawthorne related the account of a boy who had heard the legend that some day a man would appear who would resemble the image which nature had artistically carved into the giant rocks of a mountain. For years the young man made it a practice to look daily toward this great stone face and wish that the stranger would appear. Eventually, as was the case with Tokuharu Miki, the young man, now grown older, recognized himself as the promised one whose coming had been foretold.

Rensei is the fulfillment of that kind of prophecy and the embodiment of the Tokuharu Miki kind of experience. People, young people particularly, who come here for spiritual development, recognize their true identity, find within themselves new qualities made graphic at *Seichi* the art, the cleanliness, the beauty, the creativity and initiative which are everywhere expressed.

You can see the change take place. In four days a kind of miracle happens. By way of the influence of Oshieoya and Tsugioya, by the impressive ritual of *Oyashikiri*, by the dynamic force of *Makoto*, by the belief in the Twenty-one Precepts and their insistence that man's life begins and ends in self expression, PL has become for them a way of life.

■ 4 ■

From the beginning of my on-location study of PL, I was impressed by the judgment factor, the ability of the followers to sense the lasting value of an experience, the insight to know what is good for the soul and what might conceivably cause the self to be divided. It is at this point that the Twenty-one Precepts are interrelated. When judgment cautions that "all things exist in mutual relationship to one another" the idea is closely tied to the counsel that one should "comprehend what is most essential." When it is affirmed that "all things progress and develop" it becomes more meaningful to remember that one is also advised to "act when your intuition dictates." The philosophical implications of all these were to be discussed with staff members later on, but just now I was seeing them graphically demonstrated in the life of the people at Seichi.

For example, everything about Habikino suggested affluence and the metaphysical working of a "prosperity law," but one never had the impression of commercialism or a hint of money-making or money-getting or money-emphasis. On the contrary, everyone I met seemed devoid of any materialistic tendency in word or deed. You must observe this for yourself to believe it. If you look for a demonstration of the favorite Christian axiom, "Seek ye first the kingdom of God and all things will be added unto you," you are bound to find a strong hint of the operation of this truth here at PL headquarters. There is a sense of God's presence being at the heart of the program and, in the midst of a booming, inflated national economy, you find here a quiet, secure sense about the propriety of things, money included.

Judgment. The people seem to exercise judgment in the realm of values. Go into the art centers or the tea room, stroll through PL land, play the challenging golf courses, largest and finest in Japan, and you will not be annoyed by the usual tips and tricks so conventional in the business or recreational world.

Speaking of golf prompts me to include among the people who impressed me the nearly 300 teenage girls who serve as caddies on four-hour shifts, in this way paying their way through high school at Seichi. They serve from dawn to dusk seven days a week and make every game, no matter what your capability, an unforgettable match. Smartly dressed in blue slacks, orange windbreakers, wearing a white

headband plainly marked PL, these unspoiled, spirited caddiettes have an uncanny sense of just how far to go in sharing your moods and your decisions without once making
themselves intrusive.

You see them jog to the clubhouse at stated times
throughout the day. You discover them with wicker baskets methodically picking up every weed and tiny bit of
refuse during their "rest periods." You find them ready at
hand with the proper club just when you want it. Though
they magically vanish after your game is over, they become
part of a never-to-be-forgotten memory, for they paused
with you in your admiration of the distant hills, they felt
your enthusiasm when you glanced at the marble temple or
stood for a moment in wonder at the dominant Tower of
Peace.

My opinion about all this is by no means an isolated one.
An industrial executive, Noboru Inagaki, said, "The reason
I enter the competitions in spring and autumn every year is
so that I can not only play golf for itself but also to indulge
in a fresh mood. The services of the caddies of the PL
links are beyond expression. They attend to us with warm
hearts of their own accord, and speak with affection. They
are not motivated by someone else, but by their natural
dignity. Their kindness I have never met before, and it quite
overwhelms me."

Patriarch Miki commented, "Many golfers often ask the
caddies, 'What is your object in belonging to the PL religion?' The caddies usually answer without hesitation, 'Well,
it is for the public peace.' It comes to this, the more they go
heart and soul into their work, the more the road leads
nearer to the realization of a peaceful society."

In an interview with a group of PL young people, when
we were discussing *Makoto*, one of the girls said, "*Makoto*
means getting in tune with people. When I was a caddy
several years ago there was a golf player who seemed very
stern and severe. I was really a little afraid of him. He
never said anything and he always seemed to be on the other

side of a bridge from me. Then I said to myself, 'Maybe he has some heavy problems on his mind. Maybe he has come here to forget them or figure them out. I must not be afraid. I must understand him and be as good to him as I can without making him feel he must pay any attention to me.' I tried to do this and the feeling of a bridge between us disappeared. When the game was over he looked at me and said with great sincerity that my services and the game had meant more to him than I would ever know. This is *Makoto*."

There is more to the reference that PL is a "golf religion" than meets the eye. Yet the caddiettes, who made golf a great experience for a non-golfer like me, are actually no different than the young people of *Rensei* or those who serve in the tea room or the inn or who greet you in the many offices and shops. In fact, they are very often the same young people doubling on jobs. At a sumptuous formal dinner one evening I realized that the charming young lady in silken kimono and *obi* who served me *sake* with such faultless finesse was the same girl I had seen working with computers earlier in the day.

While the great crowds that come to PL to join in the festivals, to eat and shop in PL land, to attend the services and to work as volunteers on the grounds, may give you the impression that PL is for oldsters, the very opposite is closer to the truth. PL has a tremendous hold on youth. You find them in the art and science programs, in the computer analysis laboratories, and, most of all, in the ministerial training courses. All of which is why PL's future is promising and why PL's present is bright.

■ 5 ■

But the innermost secret about the people at Seichi is this: each person finds the place where his talent fits and he is therefore obviously content. Credit for this honorific situation usually goes to the Patriarch. Whenever I inquired why such-and-such a person was where he was and how he got there, the answer was simply, "Oshieoya made an opportunity for him" or "Well, that is where he fits and that is the way Oshieoya-sama understands these things."

It could conceivably go deeper than all this. True, the state of consciousness created by Patriarch Miki and the people's faith in him are largely responsible for putting the power aptitudes into the proper place, but there is also an innate willingness on the part of the people to serve wherever they feel their capabilities can best be used. Soon the master workman, be he artist or ceramist or computer expert, finds himself surrounded by apprentices who feel they are needed and wanted. In the building of the Peace Tower, students interested in becoming construction engineers, draftsmen and even steeplejacks found an opportunity to get practical training and a fresh insight into their chosen careers.

I often thought of the maxims of the Carmelite monk, Brother Lawrence, during my PL visit. He once said, "Men invent many means and methods of coming into God's love. They learn rules and set up devices and go to a world of trouble to bring themselves into a consciousness of God's presence. Yet it could be so simple. Is it not quicker and easier just to do our common business wholly for love of Him? Thus we put His consecration upon all we lay our hands to, at the same time establishing communion of our hearts with His and thereby realizing the sense of His abiding presence."

The words graphically describe PL. Here at Seichi people approach life with a sense of spiritual vocation. Here they try to live the Twenty-one Precepts as completely as possible and we really cannot fully grasp these Precepts until they *are* lived. PL headquarters provides a proving ground for testing the validity and value of such affirmations as "Live radiantly as the sun"—"Man suffers if he fails to express himself"—"Live in perfect unity of mind and matter"—"Strive for creating mutual happiness."

How these affirmations are implemented in a man's vocation was suggested forcibly by my meeting with Mr. Oda who heads up the program in plant research, gardening and landscaping. My first visit with this keen and canny botanist convinced me that he was, of course, a true prototype of Japanese gardeners whom we on the West Coast consider to be the world's finest. Here at PL, the middle-aged Mr. Oda enjoys not only the expression of his horticultural talent, but has a physical plant and seemingly unlimited resources for experimental research. He also has a staff of dedicated men and women totally committed to their jobs and to him.

When I asked this amiable craftsman whether in his thirty years experience he believed there was anything to the theory that plants respond to human emotions, my question really opened up the communication channels. Mr. Oda not only believed in the psychic ties that persisted in this field, he had experimented with the effect of *Oyashikiri* in his laboratory and had found to his satisfaction that flowers and plants are attuned to spiritual vibrations.

I had recently done some writing on the work of polygraph expert Cleve Backster who had speculated that a secret signal may connect all unicellular life and that plants conceivably feel and react to conditions around them. Not only had Mr. Oda heard of these experiments, he had been following closely the research being done in the latest meristem discoveries in the United States and France. PL built a large ultra-modern "plant laboratory," as germ free as a space module, and in it Mr. Oda and his assistants are working on such assignments as virus-free potatoes, experiments in the area of merichrome studies, and other research projects defined as closer cooperation between nature and man.

This cooperation is a basic principle evident among all the people-projects in PL whether in the development of plant life, flower arranging, arts and crafts, mechanical engineering or in the advanced areas of health and healing. Hosho-kai Byoin, the medical center at Seichi, is beginning to attract considerable attention because of its achievement in using both spiritual and medical therapies. This newly enlarged hospital is staffed by qualified medical men, many of whom are also PL ministers who deal mostly with PL patients. Mutual trust and common consciousness are vital factors in the high percentage of speed in recovery and permanence of cure.

Contributing to the advance in this spiritual-physical treatment is the rapidly expanding psychosomatic research center which, in turn, works closely with BCM (Basic Computerized Mission), the electronic nexus of PL's health and healing program which will provide data to help control the emotions. When something happens in the mind, there is a reaction or an equivalent in the body. The PL computer syndrome will define these reactions. Usually psychology only studies neuroses and then classifies types. PL is broadening the study, analyzing the classifications and charting the course of cure.

To properly understand this it must be remembered that from the very start of the patient's medical examination, spiritual factors are considered as important as the physical symptoms in the quest for health. For example, on the questionnaires will be inquiries about the patient's date of initiation into PL, the time when he received the *Omitama*, whether or not he had *Rensei* training and if so when, his requests for *Mioshie* and his class of membership in the PL movement.

One of the "Face Sheets" I examined had 160 questions and suggested that these be answered in thirty minutes. Their range and insight were bound to get at the root cause of a disease rather than a mere study of the disease itself.

Where other systems may disregard the effect of the emotions, the work at PL is an attempt, with computerized assistance, to correlate any pathological findings with disturbances of the mind and the state of the "psyche." Thus it is understandable that questions such as the following are relevant:

Is there anything you would be ashamed of, if people knew about it?

Do you mind if others whisper to each other around you?

Do you worry about what you have said?

Do you leave tasks half-finished?

Do you sometimes feel inclined to say, "I told you so"?

Do you sometimes end up with donating less than you initially intended to give?

Are you easily moved to tears?

When you have meals, do you sometimes eat your favorite food last?

Do you think you are unlucky?

Do you worry about what others think about you?

"We are studying *Mioshie,*" one of the doctors explained. "First objectively, then subjectively. For example, a patient is strong-headed. He sees this trait in others, but not in himself. Then he is taught to look at the world subjectively. Again, if a person is in too much haste, we translate this objectively, then ask that it be done subjectively.

"We do this by means of the questionnaire to show the psychological makeup of the patient. Then we take the questionnaire to the computer and make an instant quantitative analysis which includes regression analysis. The analysis is then categorized. Pontification analysis gives optimum analysis. Advice is given to the patient after analysis. This advice is equal to the *Mioshie*, but the expression is different. This is subjective. *Mioshie* is objective. Then the two are compared.

"Let's say a person is stubborn and knows it. This is conscious and will not cause *Mishirase*. But the computer should be able to detect if the person is stubborn and is *unconscious* of it. You see, the questions act as a mirror. The phenomenon around you is also a mirror. Through PL's computerized assistance we can broaden our study of neurotic types. We can handle about five hundred *Mishirases* a day. The information is sent in from ministers and we can now quickly prescribe a *Mioshie*. One of the things we are after is to measure how the human emotions affect the human body. It is often as difficult to ascertain why a person is sick as to explain what makes a girl unattractive or attractive."

The extent of PL's enormous feedback of information becomes apparent when you consider that PL has more than a million case histories to draw upon, cases involving *Mishirase* and *Mioshie* which have now been data processed! The patient, of course, has filled out both his physical questionnaire and the psychological questionnaire, and diseases, both functional and organic, have been pretty well categorized. Precipitating events which start the patient on a neurotic track and which then lead him into various functional disorders have been convincingly charted. So have various types of disease and their relation to emotional and traumatic causes. The interesting point at PL is not only in confirmation of what other psychosomatic researchers have found or in the highly specialized adjunct of computerization, but it is significant that this kind of total service should be provided by a religious denomination.

It may be argued that this has also been done by Western religions. After all, Presbyterianism, Lutheranism, Methodism, the Seventh Day Adventists and Roman Catholicism in particular have long been noted for their medical service and skills. But it is safe to say that nowhere has the actual inclusion of prayer, spiritual counsel and medicine reached the close partnership and inter-association that it has at Seichi.

Here we find medical men advocating *Oyashikiri*. Here we see *Mishirase* and *Mioshie* considered as indispensable steps in the understanding of health and healing. Doctors confirm that during operations, *Oyashikiri* definitely helps both the patient in his will to cooperate and recover, and helps the surgeon in the administration of his skills. Operations, however, are always a matter of last resort after all other therapies have not been able to correct the cause.

As a result of this synthesized approach to illnesses of all kinds, there has arisen a new concept of ministerial training in which the analysis of *Mishirase* and the divine counsel of *Mioshie* take on ultra-modern interpretations. There is now a cooperative effort involving medical practitioner, psychotherapist and clergyman, with the groundwork and inspiration of Oshieoya fundamentally a major factor in this combined healing technique.

"Oshieoya urged us to unite science and religion," a physician told me, "and that is what we are doing. We are aiming at a program of preventive medicine. We see the hospital of the future as a preventive place. We send out five thousand health sheets monthly to PL members as a means of averting sickness. Our check-up system will use the best electronic equipment. Multi-phase advice to patients will prevent illness, both physical and psychological."

PL's goal is even greater than that. It aims at a total lifetime program to aid its people in all areas so that they may better work out the assignment that "Life Is Art."

Beyond this, Oshieoya envisions the unfoldment of another dream. When the individual learns to control his will and balance his emotions, he becomes the "man of peace." Then and only then will he be equipped to usher in the era of the "Great Peace" which is PL's hope and surety for a currently troubled world. Ask the people at Seichi about this and they will turn their eyes understandingly to the Peace Tower's silent vigil on its Habikino hill.

Chapter Six

THE
PATRIARCH

I WAS IN THE great Assembly Hall at Seichi sitting with Rev. Koreaki Yano at a table in the auditorium close to the huge proscenium. It was ten o'clock on the morning of *Kyoshu-Tanjosai*, the birthday festival of Oshioya-sama.

Around us, above us in the encircling balcony, behind us, stretching out into the street were five thousand ardent followers of PL, dressed in their festive best; dignitaries, political figures, industrialists, people of Japan's workaday world, young and old, a group of Americans, delegates from Brazil, students and faculty members of the PL schools and staffs. There would be a repeat observance later in the day. The assembly auditorium would again be filled to overflowing.

The worship service had begun. The sixty-foot-long curtain, pure silk, a masterpiece of art woven in five hundred shades and colors depicting the sunrise as seen from

Mt. Ioma, had risen to reveal the spacious stage and its impressive altar above which was a golden *Omitama*, its mirror center a glowing crystal light.

Something about the *Omitama* symbol, the utter simplicity and beauty, the feeling here at Seichi, spoke of the coming of a new life-style, a new concept in religion, the advent of the creative man of a new age. Here was a prelude to a new decade and a prophetic look towards a new century.

So it seemed as some forty ministers, princely in their PL robes entered one by one to impressively invoke the blessing of *Mioya-Ookami*. Here was the ultimate in dignity and precision of which the PL services I had attended in American PL churches had been faultless reenactments. Rev. Yano and his ministers were also looking forward to what they called the new age, the new faith, the new creative man inspired by Oshieoya.

Oshieoya. He made his entrance after the ministers were seated. He entered from stage right, followed by his queenly wife, known to PL people as Kagemioya. Both were resplendent in ceremonial garments of silver and gold. Oshieoya wore a matching mitre and pure white gloves. A pontifical figure if ever I saw one, he betrayed no hint of his seventy years. Erect and courtly, he moved with priestly grace, each movement conveying the gentle hint that "Life is Art."

Later I was to meet him in person, Tokuchika Miki the Supreme Patriarch. I was also to know him as the Ambassador of Peace and as Tokuchika Miki the man, but now I was seeing him for the first time as he advanced with liturgical grace toward the *Omitama* and the altar to make his prayer. All was as I had imagined it would be, pure drama, true worship, a paradox of power and joy, but again there was this evidence of the new man for a new age.

In one of his writings he had said, "It is very well to say that one's life flows with the movement of nature and that everything that happens to us is a destiny, but man also has

94

free will. He uses this free will and wisdom to figure things out. Then adding form and creativity to his decisions, he performs a work of art. Only in this way can a human being feel happy and fulfilled."

Again there was *Oyashikiri*. It was one thing to sit up front at a service of this kind and see the white-gloved hands lifted in the symbol of the sun, but it was also thrilling to imagine what it must be like to be in the balcony gazing down on five thousand pairs of hands making the same sign and feeling the *Makoto* rising from the synchronized movements of the congregation.

The folded hands, the lifted hands, the symbol, the obeisance, the low bow, the gracious nod, the rhythm—nature and man's creativity, predeterminism and free will harmonized in idea and form. "Live in perfect unity of mind and matter!" says the Twentieth Precept.

I was beginning to understand why people were drawn to Patriarch Miki, why they trusted and believed in him, why they loved him and called him Oshieoya (divine teacher). Embodiment of a tradition, rightful successor to PL leadership, he deserved to wear the sacramental robe which he had accepted in all humility from his father, Kyoso. "I am young and must still learn virtue," he had told Kyoso thirty-four years ago. "I must still learn wisdom for I am but thirty-six years of age." Today he was seventy.

No doubt the thoughts that went through my mind were those of the worshippers around me. Tradition is precious in religion. The right of succession is powerful. Here was Oshieoya-sama who as a young student had received the blessing of the mystic Kanada. Here was a man who had suffered imprisonment with Kyoso and who had demonstrated that "life is art" even under persecution.

Tokuchika Miki had proved himself qualified through every phase of PL growth from the time that there was nothing here at Seichi but barren ground, mud and dust, summer rains and winter's cold, no temple, dormitories, gardens or lighted fountains. There was in those days just one thing: Kyoso's dream and prophecy, the founder's unshakable conviction that the faith would grow and prosper.

Just outside the Assembly Hall where we were seated was the Garden of Poetry, the original site of the founding of the PL settlement. It was here that Patriarch Miki had expressed his aspiration in traditional tanka verse which, literally translated, says, "My soul will rejoice when the citadel of art emerges from the green hills of Habikino!"

I felt the exhilaration among the people. You see, Patriarch Miki had actually shied away, after his father's imprisonment and death, from becoming the leader of the erstwhile *Hito no Michi* group. But those who loved him felt, as he did, his divine call, and after counsel received through prayer, he made the choice.

"We accept nature's movement when we make a decision," he had said, "and then we work with our decision cooperatively. God gives a man one hundred percent grace and blessing when he sheds his ego. You, not God, begin the process. Shed your ego and you receive grace. Make room for fulfillment and you will be filled. Ego means 'one with oneself.' Effacement of ego means 'one with God.' "

As he bowed before the *Omitama* and the enchanted hush fell over the worshipers, as I caught the deep sincerity of Rev. Yano standing beside me, I remembered a question I had put to a young PL minister. He had spoken so affectionately and uncritically about *Oshieoya* that I was compelled to ask, "Would you say you have deified him? Has the Patriarch become a kind of god for you?"

I remembered how the young man looked at me, how he showed concern as he turned my question over in his mind, then how he laughed lightly and replied, "You do not understand. We are *all* made in the image of God. We are all deified. Oshieoya would be amused if we said he was more God than we are. We have a precept that says, 'All men are equal.' But when a person loves more, as does the Patriarch, we love the person more because he is giving us more love to love with. You understand? When a person shows more talent for things, we appreciate him more because he stirs up talents in us. When he is more self-sacrificing, we admire him more because we know there is more in us that we can do if only we will try."

A PL follower said to me, "The presence of Oshieoya is everywhere, but I am happy to be at Seichi because I feel nearer to him here. It is good to see him, to see him smile, and to hear him whenever he speaks. He always makes me want to be better than I am."

The five thousand worshipers in the Assembly Hall would unquestioningly agree. Two million followers, many of whom have never seen him in person, would no doubt voice the same opinion. They study his books, especially his popular *Life Is Art*, a best seller in Japan. They are moved by his poetry. They stand in quiet admiration before his ideograms. They listen to his recorded messages and watch him on film. They would see him as we were seeing him now at worship, for in this moment of *Kyoshu-Tanjosai*, inconspicuous but expert cameramen were filming each episode of the colorful scene as the Patriarch did *Oyashikiri* and on to the final gesture when he turned to the people, spread his arms in the luxurious folds of his golden vestment, lifted his gloved hands and pronounced a blessing.

Through Rev. Koreaki Yano standing with bowed head and from the empathic flow of those around me, I knew how great their fervor was for this spiritual leader. He had divine insight in which they trusted and believed. He was a symbol of their better selves, an inspiration to their highest good, a trusted guide along their way.

Surely they remembered how he said, "It is very well to say that everything that happens to us is destiny, but man also has free will. He uses this free will and wisdom to figure out things. Then, adding form and creativity to his decisions, he performs a work of art. Only in this way can a human being feel happy and fulfilled."

■ 2 ■

Then there was Tokuchika Miki the Ambassador for Peace.

To be a pontifical figure, a Supreme Patriarch, is one thing. To prove oneself a leader in an international world cause is quite another. Here at the birthday observance the prevailing mission of Miki's life became clear: world peace is his passion.

This was graphically demonstrated when he next appeared on the stage of the Assembly Hall to be greeted by state and industrial dignitaries and to acknowledge and honor the good wishes of various PL officials. He had changed from his canonicals into a dignified kimono attire which seemed to combine the influence of East and West. Here he was, a wholesome, easy-to-meet, buoyantly enthusiastic lover of life concentrating on a major role: envoy for the "Great Peace."

His formal remarks were built around this theme. His references were so close to so much of my thinking that I was completely captivated. Rev. Yano, leaning across the table translating Miki's words, may have wondered why I kept nodding agreement. It was because the speaker was expounding on my favorite theme: the essential unity of all religions, the need for spiritual cooperation in order to drive the scourge of war from the scarred face of God's good earth. How often had the thought occurred to me that we cannot have a united world while we have divided faiths! How many times had I speculated that most conflicts have as their justification the rationalization of a holy war, a divine right to destroy and kill! Now here was a man launching a crusade for peace built upon the spirit of God in the life of man!

What greater theme? What more urgent thesis? What more forceful subject than to remind the world once more that men must learn to live together if they are to live at all and that as the ego of man must be effaced so must the ego of nations!

Tokuchika Miki, ambassador for all who knew with all their heart that war is obsolete and never holy, was speaking at a time when the missiles of Russia were targeted at the United States and those of the U.S.A. were aimed with equal accuracy at the U.S.S.R. His words were being broadcast at the very time that China was impressively forging its way into the atomic race. Japan had just launched its first satellite. Southeast Asia was a bloody battlefield. The Judeo-Christian-Moslem "Holy Land" was poised at the crossroads of crisis. He was pleading with humanity at a point in history when brushfire wars were plaguing the globe, when gunfire was drowning the voices for tolerance, and when the logic of force had all but silenced the logic of love. He was urging, as every genuine spiritual leader always has, what I have called an ecumenicity of the spirit. Committed to a religion of his own, he was more committed to a religion of all mankind, and this to me was memorable. This approach was different. He was no longer a sectarian Patriarch but an ambassador-at-large, ready to invoke a summit meeting of spiritual leaders to see what creative breakthroughs might be found to put an end to man's most stubborn lust.

It became clear as I listened to Rev. Yano's translation of the impassioned address that Tokuchika Miki looked upon the PL movement as a demonstration in microcosm of the workability of the "Great Peace" on a global scale. When he stated that "man is a manifestation of God, but God is not man, and man is not God Himself," he was graphically emphasizing that world peace is impaired whenever an individual sets himself up as God or vaunts his ego over his fellow-man.

Granted that a human being is God's noblest creation, that man alone possesses the capabilities and the artistic expression to create a warless world, Miki wanted to make sure that his people understood that "the human being's unique position is not unconditional."

"The life of man," he warned, "is a constant struggle between inevitable limitations and a desire for the unlimited. Man's limitations are apparent in his intellectual abilities, his physical capabilities, his spiritual perception. What makes man the noblest of all creatures is his conscious desire to overcome and surmount these limitations."

So it is with man's hitherto incapacity to usher in the era of peace and goodwill. But the past reach of man's capability is not the limit of the capability. PL is a proving ground, a laboratory for the development of limitless potentials.

"How," Miki asked, "can a natural expression of self help to be anything but selfish or self-centered?" He answered his question by way of a PL decree: "Your natural self-expression cannot be selfish if you have a clear understanding of your relative position with your fellowman, society, God, and the Divine Universal Plan. Life Is Art. Man's life is a struggle to overcome his limitations. Art is not an escape. It is a constructive and positive step forward."

Such was the gist of the microcosm. Such was the plan, and since it had been tested and proved in the PL order, Miki felt justified in offering it as a blueprint for world understanding.

"When we say that 'Life Is Art,' " he explained, "we mean that each individual should express his unique personality given by God, but always in relationship to the Divine Plan and always in reference to the Great Peace. This is true *Makoto*. This is *Makoto* unlimited for world peace. At that point where individual, home, group, race, nation, all express rightly their unique character, there lies the way to world

100

understanding. The purpose of our teaching is to heartfully enjoy the only life in this world by expressing dependence upon God and working for the welfare and peace of humanity. For this it is necessary that we all work together. I beg for this your sincere cooperation."

Understandably the audience rose to its feet to acknowledge their enthusiasm for their leader's views. In the intermission that followed—it was noon now and with effortless expertise PL workers fed the five thousand with box luncheons—there was much conversation across the tables and by small groups commenting on how PL was assuming leadership in an inter-religious, inter-cultural movement for peace. Tokuchika Miki had a plan for enlisting the youth of the world, inviting them to come to *Seichi* to learn to live together and express the artistry of life.

No one spoke about this phase of PL more clearly than Tsugioya, successor to Patriarch Miki, who had greeted me at the Palace on the night of my arrival. Tsugioya, director of the international youth program, had this to say about the international youth program, had this to say about Oshieoya's quest for peace:

"The dream and desire of our Patriarch is at last coming true. Since the dawn of history, mankind, while constantly desiring peace, has wept at the horror of war and has been frustrated by hostilities. The purpose of Perfect Liberty is the Great Peace. We are now calling on all PL youth members and on all of the world's young people to join us, to cry out that today's youth must know that in the background of history innumerable cases of holy sacrifices must now be accounted for, and that it is the young generation of all nations who must concentrate their strength and advance toward building world peace."

This expression of Tsugioya became especially significant when the birthday observance resumed. The program featured a festival of traditional Japanese dances by some of the country's most famous exponents of the art, and several impressive numbers by students of the PL school of the dance. The hour-long presentation was all too short, for the sheer delight of traditional folk sequences, the striking performances of classical numbers, the virtuosity of masters whom Miki had invited to share in the program, held us spellbound.

Yet all was merely prologue to what was an unexpected display of consummate artistry by Tokuchika Miki himself who, with his wife, presented an amazingly prophetic "Peace Tower Dance."

This special performance featured choreography around a fourteen-foot replica of the PL Peace Tower which rose out of the stage floor with arresting technical effect. Here was Tokuchika Miki in fascinating makeup, like a *kabuki* player, stunningly costumed, fan in hand, enacting with his partner Kagemioya the saga of the memorial and inviting the people of the world to make it their rallying point for the Great Peace.

I learned later that Miki's actorial and dancing talents are taken as a matter of course. "Each year he performs an original dance at his birthday observance," I was told, "and it is understandable that this year he should choose the Peace Tower as a theme."

The dance was Miki's interpretation of the peaceable kingdom as he foresaw it in the coming century. He sought to portray the symbology of the Tower from the time he conceived it to its dedication and the fulfillment of his dream.

All of this was of special interest to me because my recent tour of the Tower was fresh in my mind. I recalled how the structure had impressed me the night I first came to Seichi. I remembered how gigantic it appeared from a distance when I walked to it the following day, how its awesome magnitude seemed to be withheld until I was near enough to realize that what I thought was a smooth and simple obelisk is actually a highly eccentric and multi-sided work of sculptured art. Perhaps Miki was saying in his dance that peace will be like that with all its multi-sided people!

My thoughts went back to my walk around the Tower, and how I agreed with my guide that no two areas of this impressionistic creation are alike and that every glance revealed a new concept in the asymmetry of construction. It could be that peace, too, should by no means have but one face! At any rate, as I watched the "Peace Tower Dance" I kept reading my own symbolism into it, remembering how I had the feeling that the Tower was surely a solid monolith, but when I entered it, I was enchanted by the wonder of its inner space, its inner freedom. Again, an intriguing commentary on the Great Peace to come!

The "Peace Tower Dance" and the Peace Tower in reality blended in my mind. I was reminded that when I stepped through the portals of the towering giant, I felt I was in the narthex of a cathedral of all faiths, and when I was told there would be a museum, an assembly hall, and rooms for PL peace activities, I was not surprised. Tens of thousands of iron bars crisscrossed at various heights, tons of steel and welded girders, twenty-four openings at various levels, an observation platform at the Tower's center, miles of wiring, tiers of metal tubing, elevator shafts, pillars clothed in concrete, and eventually the "finger of peace" pointing to the sky, this was overpoweringly real, and now here on stage reality and art mingled to portray man's perpetual dream. This was the symbolism, this the message brought to us in the magic of the dance by Oshieoya, Ambassador of Peace.

■ 3 ■

Then there was Tokuchika Miki the man. The practical man. "So the Peace Tower costs over five million dollars. Is this much when compared with one piece of military aircraft, one day of modern warfare, one count of casualties?

is any price too great to rally nations and the world in the cause of peace?"

The man of action and sentiment. "I have served as director of the Union of New Religions of Japan, as Commissioner to the Council of Religious Corporations, as President of the Federation of Japanese Religions and so on. My first visit to the Imperial Palace was when the ceremonial of instituting the Prince Imperial was held. How glad my father would have been if he had been alive then!"

The man with a poet's heart. "The false charges of impiety under which my father suffered with heart-rending grief for so long have been wiped away, clear as the pure blue heavens. My father Kyoso, how glad he would have been!

> He became the son of the Sun
> As the symbol
> Of the land of the sun.
>
> To the throne of Japan
> Mounted the founder
> As the symbol of Japan.
>
> To drive to the Prince's banquet
> Over the Double Bridge,
> Taking good care of etiquette.
>
> To attend the Prince's feast
> Over the Double Bridge,
> No one thought of it in the least."

The philosopher. "A person bound by habits is not free. To be free one must get rid of his captives. A guard who must watch over his prisoners is fully as much a captive as they. Perfect Liberty aims at being habit-free."

The ethicist. "A man who has no interest in competition has lack of will. There is an imperative need for expressing will which is given by God to man. There is a meaning to living, and pleasure in the expression of the will deepens and develops that meaning."

The counselor. "It is necessary to use emotion to develop

a finer emotion, that is, to use it as material for your highest expression. Govern your emotion. Do not let your emotion govern you. Make your emotion into an art."

The adventurer. "Approach your situations without preconceptions. There is no true joy of creation when we simply stereotype a former action. There is joy of life when we are inspired to add a new creative touch and do things differently. Surely this is one way to keep life from becoming monotonous!"

The realist. "Do not envy those who belong to exclusive golf clubs! We will provide golf courses for you, the finest in the land. Relate the principles of golf to life. Live for the satisfaction of an artistic life."

The moralist. "When an expression has individuality it has value. When it has not, it has no value worthy of art. Art remains uncreated if we only feel it in our hearts or hold it in imagination. Nothing can be art until it is expressed."

The man of intuition. "You are a manifestation of God. The best way to respond to life is to observe your first impression. The first impression means the first reaction of the senses. It is the intention of God to teach us rightly which way we should go. It must be an intuition. The more you rely upon the first impression, the sharper it becomes. The more you develop it the more you will live your life in accordance with nature, peacefully and properly."

The man of the world. "My self is not for myself, it is rather for others. It is a constitutional part of society. I should not express myself by ignoring others. Only as there is harmony with others does the self become an instrument for world peace. Secluding yourself, living as a hermit in the mountains, this is more like an animal than a man. There is no social value if you live apart from social life. Our lives are interwoven with other lives, we are dependent upon one another. But always we are unique. We are individuals. Real peace will come when we understand this true relationship."

Yet, what was he like, Tokuchika Miki the man? Behind

the sayings, the philosophizing, the artistry, what was he like when he stepped from the aura of the stage and was no longer the cynosure of thousands of devoted followers? What happens when a leader loses the benefit of the psychological distance between himself and his people? When, as we say, the public figure has no prepared script and when the image makers have left him on his own, what is he like? Patriarch, Ambassador of Peace, whatever the title, what is the man?

You can, of course, get some good impressions from those who have worked closely with him and who have known him all their lives, who have been in and out of his presence and are sufficiently objective to make their own appraisals.

Rev. Koreaki Yano was such a one and he was of the opinion Oshieoya was a man of tremendous balance, balance of insight and action, faith and work, humility and power, a man equal to any achievement he resolved on, and a man with a commitment to honor his destiny as a spiritual leader and leave his world better and more at peace than he had found it.

Rev. Kingo Inamura, director of the Arts Seminar and secretary in the office of the Patriarch, had the benefit of learning both English and the style of Western life in the United States. This young man, a skilled linguist, felt that he had never been in the presence of Oshieoya without receiving inspiration for higher values in life.

"He is such a man," said Inamura, "that he equalizes everything and puts things into their proper perspective. He has great insight. He has helped many young people find their vocations in life, doctors of medicine or computer experts because he saw their qualifications. But one of the reasons I respect him most is because he is humble in the eyes of God. He does not claim he knows everything, but what he knows he applies to life."

Donald Steele's evaluation of Miki the man was of special

interest. "The Patriarch," he said, "is a very human person who has developed his power of perception and his ability to generate what might be called mystic abilities in the ESP range of qualities and values. He has helped many associated with him to build up their ability to help others and to adjust their lives in times of misfortune, illness or bad luck. It seems to me that his objective and the goal of PL is to create a breed of humans all over the world who discover their individuality, their true self, and learn to live together under the credo that 'Life Is Art.' "

My own curiosity about the man was satisfied during opportune meetings both "on stage" and off, and especially at an informal evening dinner which he hosted for Mrs. Bach and me and for the Steeles at a room in the Palace. On this occasion Patriarch Miki was accompanied by his exquisitely beautiful daughter, Shirahi, a respected poet and talented artist in her own right. Her lovely Japanese attire and the Patriarch's modest Western-style business suit were a happy indication of the harmony between Eastern and Western culture. In fact, even the low, polished rosewood tables and chairs seemed a gracious concession to Americans who find it uncomfortable to sit Oriental fashion on *tatami* mats.

The ten guests were Rev. Tokuhito Miki (Tsugioya) and his charming wife, Mr. and Mrs. Donald Steele, Rev. Koreaki Yano, Professor Toshio Yasaka, Rev. Kingo Inamura, a special interpreter Mr. Bungo Ishizaki, Mrs. Bach and I. The seating arrangement convinced me that life can be art even in planning a practical way for twelve people to eat together (see illustration on the following page).

This table planning left ample freedom for the gracious serving of the ten-course meal by a group of youthful PL girls in silken kimonos and *obi* sashes, carefully directed by the Palace's efficient housekeeper, Mrs. Sadako Sugimura.

These PL "waitresses," by the way, were young employees and assistants in Seichi offices and doubled on many jobs. Ever attentive and never intrusive, they now added joy and

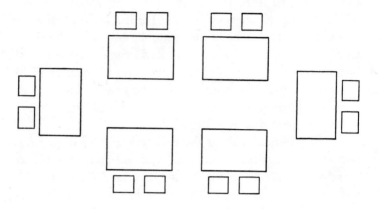

beauty to the magic of the Japanese cuisine in the won-
drously cheerful atmosphere of this eight-to-ten-o'clock
festive meal. In fact, we stayed until after midnight, largely
because of the gracious willingness of Patriarch Miki to re-
count many important details of the history, philosophy and
goals of the Perfect Liberty movement.

I was particularly interested in his viewpoint when, in
answer to my question about the relationship between the
spiritual and economic growth in Japan, he said he did not
think there was the close analogy which some religious
scholars attached to this dual phenomenon. It would be difficult, he felt, to say which came first: Japan's will to work
or its wish to worship, but to infer that the country was
prospering economically because its people were unduly
"religious" would give a distorted impression and a false
hope.

He was of the opinion that people were basically the

same all around the world. The PL precept that "all men are equal" by no means applied only to Japan! It pertained to all humanity and implied that the Self is universally the expression of God. So, too, the Fourteenth Precept that "All is for world peace" could not achieve its goal if restricted only to Japanese people. Peace is everybody's business. "All" meant everyone and everything. It meant man's efforts, resources, thinking, work, and dreams.

Tokuchika Miki the man was of the opinion that people are inherently good. All are born with *Makoto* (sincerity, devotion), but it is not enough to let it go at that. *Makoto* should be improved and developed as one matures, and this development should be aimed at peace within oneself and in the world.

The individual should think in terms of improving the work of God. It is all very well to praise and glorify God for His wonders of creation, but man has been placed on earth to work cooperatively with God in the development and beautification of the world.

"I admire the Christian ethic of dedicated work," he said, "and the spirit of the pilgrims who came to America and developed new frontiers. To make work an act of God is admirable. The Japanese, too, are hard working and sincere because of an ethnic characteristic, a Shinto principle of working with nature. They have pride in work."

Pride, Mr. Miki reflected, has both a favorable and an unfavorable side. It is exemplary when tempered by *Makoto*, by sincerity, honesty, and so on. It is unfavorable when accompanied by arrogance and lack of respect for the rights of others. The prerequisite for the good life is the awareness of the unity of man and a cosmic power.

The thought occurred to me that it would be interesting, though perhaps presumptuous, if I were to ask the girls who had so expertly served us just what *they* thought of Tokuchika Miki and what impressed them most about him. Through the sensitive interpretation of Mr. Ishizaki my wish was transmitted to Oshieoya. He laughed good-naturedly and exclaimed, "Why not? Come, girls, our guest has a question for you. What do you think of Patriarch Miki?"

The sixteen girls, lovely, confident, full of spirit, yet with a touch of shyness, assembled in the open space between the tables where they sat in Oriental fashion.

"What impresses you most about the Patriarch?" asked Mr. Ishizaki.

"I worked my way through school as a caddy," was the first reply, "and I was impressed by the adaptability of Mr. Miki under all circumstances in playing golf. He was adaptable to all situations at all times. This was helpful to me."

"When I saw the Patriarch's humility," another spoke up, "I was drawn to him. More and more I wanted to cast all human or ego feeling out of myself."

"I was a Buddhist," a girl testified. "I had to chant Buddhist *sutras* and think in terms of a leader who is no longer living. The meaning of the *sutras* was lost, whereas when I came here I realized that Oshieoya is a *living* leader. This meant much to me."

Quietly a girl reflected, "What impresses me is how the influence of Mr. Miki changes lives. Lives he has changed have had an effect on me when I came here to PL. I worked in a kitchen and I was very awkward. One day I dropped a cup and it broke. At home I would have been scolded and made ashamed at what I had done. Here when it happened a superior said to me, 'Perhaps you did not have your mind on your work. Remember that and you will do all right.' I never forgot that. Maybe the Patriarch is saying this to all of us, 'Keep your mind on your work, you will do all right.'"

"I have been here for fifteen months," a lovely wisp of a girl spoke up. "I came here because of my parents' great respect for the Patriarch and PL. Everyone tells me I have changed a great deal. I do not realize any change only that I am much happier than I have ever been."

"My greatest feeling about the Patriarch," another girl explained, "is that he gives us *Mioshie*, that is, he tells us the reason for our misfortune and how we can profit from the things that have happened to us."

"I have a confession to make," said a girl shyly with a light laugh. "I feel that other young people, even those who are in PL, are somewhat underprivileged because they do not have the closeness to the person of the Patriarch that we have, we who are here at Daihoncho (headquarters compound)."

There were other impressive testimonies. Miss Shirahi, daughter of the Patriarch, spoke of him as one who could not be put into a mold because he always surprised her by enacting another, unexpected role.

The wife of Tsugioya said, "I am inspired by the Patriarch because of his trustworthiness. I admire him for his humanity. I appreciate him for his artistry. I am grateful to him for his leadership. He is like a beacon and helps me to stay on the right course."

Patriarch Miki, reflecting on all that had been said, sat with a look of fatherly love and calm as if every speaker was part of his household and important in his own quest for truth. Then he laughed quietly and said, "You know, just now I feel like the elephant in the story when the blind persons described his ears, his trunk, his body. . . . Many of the things you feel you have found in me are, of course, discoveries within yourself."

It was a significant note on which to end the evening, but it was not quite the end, for after we had said our *sayonaras* and when the Patriarch and his daughter had driven away to their home, Rev. Koreaki Yano came into the room where a group of us were still visiting. In his quiet way he said, "Come outside to see a beautiful sight."

It was an understatement, for out across the PL terrain an incredible display of colored lights and a panoply of dancing water had gone into action in the illuminated fountain fronting the white marble temple. The effect was indescribable, especially since the thrust of the main geysers is said to be the highest (seventy feet) and most spectacular in a country noted for its dramatic fountain effects. When the geysers rose and receded, hundreds of small fountains pirouetted in the ever changing iridescence while the alabaster *Seiden* with its golden *Omitama* stood emblazoned in the play of colors and mist. We stood enthralled. It was one of the first occasions when the full ensemble of the fountain had performed its magic in the shadow of Daiheiwato, the Tower of Peace.

That Tokuchika Miki had been thoughtful enough to surprise and honor us with this spectacle told us a great deal about the man. Perhaps all he had to do was give the order and it may have been a little thing, but little things like this are the telltale signs of greatness.

In fact, I have never quite figured out the secret of charisma. Some people have it, others do not, and how much of it is due to "little things" or how much is in the eye of the beholder only deepens the mystery.

We may carry the mirror of charismatic reflection within ourselves more deeply than we know and the emanation supposedly from others may be our own.

Whatever it is, however it is generated, some people have it and those around them catch it and feel it, as everyone feels sunshine and warmth, even those who are blind. Charisma, I am sure, is generated in part by the universal touch of love, inner joy, and compassion.

How great the love of those who have love to spare! How abundant the inner joy of those who give the impression that joy is inexhaustible! How compassionate the compassion of those who walk the world touching hearts as if they sensed the deepest longing, the secret sorrow, the highest hope, and through a charismatic touch are saying, "I understand and all is well."

Chapter Seven

THE PL
PRINCIPLES

■ 1 ■

THE PRECEPTS OF PL are inseparable from the writings of Patriarch Miki. The Principles are the practical extension of his life and thought into the lives of his people.

This becomes increasingly clear as we proceed deeper into the PL program. The influence of Oshieoya is everywhere This is not to say that he rules out the creative expression of his ministers and staff; on the contrary, the openness of his nature inspires and elicits originality from them. He has an innate ability to tap the inventive potential in others and to respect and guide their discoveries in the light of his authority and knowledge of the faith.

His commentaries on both Precepts and Principles form the basis of interpretation and waste no time in urging people to put them into practice. When I suggested to a coworker of Oshieoya that Miki has a "psychic sense" in relating PL teachings to our workaday world, just as he has an extrasensory insight into the personal needs of his people, he was inclined to agree. I predicted that when PL gets into the mainstream of Western thinking, our American "idea men" no less than our religious leaders will rapidly appropriate his insights and freely quote his constructive views. For how could any practical-minded American fail to respond to such innovative suggestions as:

"Life is interesting because it is competitive—One who has no interest in competition has lack of will—Work is done more effectively if handled rhythmically—Even the most trifling job can be made into a work of art—When your work is worship your labor is well done—The more deeply you thrust your knife into nature, explore it and study it, the more you find the greatness, delicacy and mystery of the Divine—Pain and agony are the result of disharmony with life—That which is around me is waiting to be created by me—Troubles are material to be used for pleasure and growth—There are no uninteresting things—He can do anything admirably who can grasp the center of meaning—*Oneself is the manifestation of God!*"

By way of best-selling books, illustrative material, poetry and works of art, Oshieoya continues to provide an ever broadening base for this evolving faith. To be influenced by all this, no matter how little or how much, will seem inappropriate only to those who insist upon keeping religion completely theological and doctrinaire. PL is headed toward the time when the future becomes the present, when religion becomes less formalized and more a part of life, less institutionalized and more personally involved, when belief will be the surest kind of knowledge, and faith an awareness of truth instinctively known. In the light of this I can understand PL's eagerness to have more and more creative channeling through Oshieoya and those who work closely with him. Here is a search for a new kind of spiritual vitality. Here is a quest for ideas that can be distilled and evaluated as if they *were* physically inspired.

Add to this a highly sophisticated computerized testing of the Patriarch's words and deeds to determine their functional effectiveness in the personal well-being of PL followers no less than in personal relations, and you can see why the PL movement is on the march. The object is to blend religious thought with scientific skills to give a new dimension to both the inner and the outer man, or, if you wish, to man and his environmental world.

■ 2 ■

When we examine the various levels of PL's religious and philosophical structure, we find that as there are Twenty-one Precepts representing the basic doctrine, so there are also Twenty-one Basic Principles which serve as a code of conduct and a set of moral obligations for daily living. These Principles are so direct and simple that no one can possibly escape their challenge or miss their ultimate meaning.

While the Precepts lend themselves to a wide range of philosophical interpretations, the Principles are in the form of pledges that form *a priori* to everyone professing to follow the PL way. As Oshieoya takes an oath of commitment to God and his people, so, in a very real sense, the people who daily live the Principles are fulfilling their oath to God and Oshieoya.

Compared with Christian beliefs, the Precepts might be considered as "Beatitudes," and the Principles special injunctions as straightforward as the admonitions, "Turn the other cheek," "Judge not that ye be not judged," or "Walk the second mile." We realize this when we review the Twenty-one Basic Principles (officially called *Shinko Seikatsu Kokoroe*) and think of tnem in terms of techniques for daily living.

115

Principle 1 states unequivocally:

> I will express *Makoto* (truth and sincerity) in all that
> I do and say. I will take scrupulous care in every
> phase of my life.

Principle 2 requires that:

> I will be creative and resourceful. I will look for
> shortcomings in my own thinking and action before
> feeling or expressing discontent about people or
> things.

As has been said, Patriarch Miki has written literally hundreds of commentaries and case histories to help his people understand the *Mishirase, Mioshie, Misasage* and the *Makoto* inferences involved in each and every Principle. The Oriental teaching technique which employs analogies and the lore of folk tales is skillfully handled by Oshieoya in an effort to underline the message. Often, as the saying has it, he tells people what they already know but didn't know they knew it. Which, he admits, is true of his continual reminder that, *"Oneself is the manifestation of God."*

As an example of a supportive vignette, take, for instance, Principle 3:

> I will live with sincere gratitude to God, to men,
> and to all things.

Here is how Oshieoya clinches the point with a homespun parable out of Japanese lore:

> Once upon a time there lived an old man who used to
> say, "Thank God, thank God."
>
> Even when it rained day after day and many
> complained about the weather, he said, "If we had all
> the rain at once we would be flooded. Thank God,
> He gives us the rain little by little."
>
> Then his wife fell ill and the neighbors thought that
> no matter how thankful the old man might be he
> would surely be stumped by this event.

They visited him only to find him saying, "Thank God, thank God!"

The neighbors reproached him in strong tones, "Are you such a fool as to thank God because your wife has fallen ill?" they asked.

The old man smiled and said, "Until this ripe old age my wife has taken good care of me, and now it is my turn to take care of her. God has given me a chance to make some return for her kindness. If this is not a thing for which to be grateful, what then shall I thank God for?"

The neighbors walked away with wonder in their hearts. And due to his devoted nursing, his wife made a miraculous recovery.

In view of the Patriarch's graphic use of illustrations, PL people can hardly approach the Principles without making up their own descriptive parables or finding in their own lives case histories to reinforce the various admonitions.

The reason I feel so sure about this is because on several occasions of late I have been using the Principles in sensitivity sessions among college students. I suggest that the participants select one or more of the basic statements and then give a supporting illustration either out of their own experience or by way of a relevant incident or event.

For example, I said, "Principle Four suggests that 'I WILL WORK FOR THE SAKE OF OTHERS AND WILL LIVE BY THE SPIRIT OF MISASAGE (devotion).' What analogy or episode does this bring to your mind?"

A young man in the group said, "When I am asked to work for the sake of others, I think of Nicolas Herman. He was a Frenchman who for many years floated around trying to find himself. He was a student, a workman, and then a soldier. He was wounded in war and later had a spiritual awakening which made him decide to practice what he called the presence of God. He joined a monastery and did all kinds of menial work with such a wonderful spirit that his attitude changed people's lives. When they asked him how he could work so happily for the sake of others he said, 'My time of work is no different from my time of prayer. In God's service I do my kitchen work. With God I tend the oven or scrub the floor. I pick up straws from the ground for love of Him.' Few people recognize him by the name of Nicolas Herman, because everyone knows him by his spiritual name Brother Lawrence. I think he lived PL's Principle Number Four."

So we played the game, going down the list of the Basic Principles.

> Principle 5. I will not become angry or enraged.
> Principle 6. I will not be self-opinionated or stubborn.
> Principle 7. I will be without haste, anxiety, and without pessimism regarding myself, other people, or other matters.
> Principle 8. I will not think of cheating or being unfair.

For every Principle someone always had an illustration. So did I when we came to Principle 9:

> I will not be greedy or avaricious.

In this connection I recalled a rather famous but little-known incident out of American history. It had to do with a Jewish financier during the time of the American Revolution, a man named Haym Salomon. Haym was a poor immigrant who came from Poland and opened a small and struggling brokerage office in Philadelphia. He had a lamp outside his house and even though he could barely afford the oil, he kept the light burning day and night. His wife, Rachel, said to him, "Why all this extravagance? It is luxury enough to burn the light at night, but why do it in the daytime, too?" Haym said, "It is a good sign, Rachel. People in the city are already saying, 'Things must be going well with that Jewish broker. He can afford to keep his light

118

burning day and night.' " It is a fact of history that without the financial help of Haym Salomon who became a very successful and rich man, the struggle for independence might not have been won, for he gave his fortune to the cause of freedom.

Principle 10. I will live in perfect harmony with my spouse.

Principle 11. Realizing that my child is a child of God, I will raise him to be a worthy person to men and society, and perceiving the fact that a child is a mirror of his parents, I will not dote upon my child to satisfy my own emotions.

Principle 12. I will get up pleasantly in the morning.

The Western mind will take a second glance at this Principle and say, "Well, this is surely a new inclusion in a code to live by! The Patriarch must have a sense of humor!" For getting up "pleasantly" in the morning is the subject of many good-natured jokes and quips in every home and on every commuter's train.

Oshieoya does have a sense of humor, but he also has some interesting thoughts on this "rise and shine" Principle. He is of the opinion that we need to train ourselves to get up because it is the first new step in our life each day. He believes the ability to snap into action upon getting up is practical training for making quick decisions during the day.

"When we are able to step forth at once," says Oshieoya, "our life becomes splendid surely! Those who achieve this ability are able to quickly translate ideas into action. It is not the hour that presents the problem, it is the person. Those who resist rising at five will find the same resistance at six or seven. The time we awake is the time God wakes us up!"

"Very well, Oshieoya, but what if we go to bed at ten and wake up at twelve?"

"Then," says Miki with a smile, "you may fall asleep again, for it is too early. But you might well say a prayer such as 'Dear God, pardon me if I sleep again. Please wake me at five.' If you continue to do so for several nights, you are sure to awake at five. But even though you awake at six in spite of all efforts, be in good humor and believe that it is the time of God's appointing. Generally speaking, God makes comfortable for us all that we are compelled to do!"

And, generally speaking, who has not experienced the reward of an early morning meditation before the world awakes, or a quiet walk in nature or on city streets, or the thrill of creative work and thought and nearness to God before the day-scene comes to life?

> Principle 13. I will not complain about food nor will I be particular about what I eat. I will refrain from irregular eating, overeating, and excessive drinking.
> Principle 14. I will not be idle or lazy. While working, I will not have grievances nor will I have dissatisfaction about things other people do.
> Principle 15. I will not indulge excessively in any matter.
> Principle 16. I will not be boisterous nor will I allow myself the attitude of self-importance.
> Principle 17. I will not do or say things that will offend others.

In a talk with Rev. Koreaki Yano, he explained that there was a belief in old Shinto that words have their individual spirits. Consequently when we deal with Principle 17 there is the wider implication of a spirit force at work, the hint of an emanation inherent in what we say. There is a parallelism here which we Christians may have overlooked. We have heard innumerable times that, "Thy Word is Spirit," "The Word is Life." But the principle 17 of PL and the *kotodama* of the Shinto faith have escaped us unless we take into consideration the divine, invariable power hidden in the spoken word.

It occurred to me that as the mirror is a symbol of our seeing the world as a reflection of our subjective experience, so the echo of the words we speak is a symbol of our hearing subjectively the things we consciously and unconsciously say. If what we see is in the eye of the beholder, what we hear could well be in the ear of the listener.

However it may be, what religions are driving at and what PL is reiterating is that deep within the substrata of life is the exciting world of spirit. The *kotodama* world. While every faith may have its own name for this world and this phenomenon, the reality of it is One and words are more powerful than we realize.

That this mystical application applies to thoughts as well is suggested in Principle 18: "I will not *think* in a manner that will be unkind, degrading or disrespectful to others."

Principle 19. I will always remember to "*hosho*."

Hosho is to PL what benevolent giving is to Christianity. It is not tithing exactly, for *hosho* does not think of percentage giving, but rather in terms of self-dictated love-offerings. PL provides special "treasure bags" or envelopes in which the devotee faithfully deposits his money, sends it to the church or to Seichi, or takes it to his house of worship on the twenty-first of each month at a time designated as a "Thanksgiving" service.

An American woman, a nisei, told me about her experience with the *hosho* principle. She had moved to Japan at an early age. As she grew to adulthood she began doing *hosho* even though she was not a PL member at the time. She merely believed in the concept of spiritual giving. As she made her offerings she became aware of unlooked-for blessings and a new sense of order coming into her life. After her marriage to a Japanese they left Japan to make their home in the United States. Among the belongings she disposed of before leaving Tokyo was a sewing machine which the purchaser promised to pay for in monthly installments. The woman requested that the purchaser make the payments not to her, but give them instead to a PL church in Japan as her continuing *hosho*.

The first few months in America were in remarkably good order. Jobs were scarce but in filling out an application for a library card, she impressed a supervisor so much by her handwriting that she was offered a position as a lettering clerk. She and her husband needed a new car but could hardly afford one. The car company they contacted sent a Japanese salesman who happened to have been a classmate of her brother. This resulted in an exceptionally good deal. So things continued in perfect order for some time. Then came reverses. For months everything went wrong. Mystified at what had thrown her life out of rhythm, our nisei friend learned that the purchaser of the sewing machine back in Japan had not been keeping *hosho* in accordance with the promise.

Could this, she wondered, have caused the growing series of "bad breaks"? The thought remained in her mind and she decided to reactivate her *hosho* practice in a local church. Upon doing this, things almost immediately righted themselves. What she called "the good rhythm of life" returned. Nothing could dissuade her from the belief that there is a spiritual connection between giving and receiving.

> Principle 20. I will make efforts to introduce new members to PL.
> Principle 21. I will always remember the grace of God and Oshieoya.

It is a cardinal PL teaching that "without a thankful heart, we never live a truly religious life." Nor are we given the grace of God unless we are sincere in our devotion to the Basic Principles. This is where Oshieoya plays an especially important role.

According to PL teaching and belief, human beings by

nature have the capability of "divine apprehension," that is, uncommon insight into the meaning and direction of life. We all have this ability but not everyone fully develops it. Oshieoya, however, through his intensive training as a priest, his self-discipline and his heightened innate endowment, possesses this insight to a supernormal degree. He has the talent to divine why *Mishirase* assails his people, why people become unhappy, why God's warnings are given. He knows what Principles the individual is neglecting or glossing over, and how happiness and the rhythm of life can be restored.

Oshieoya transmits *Mioshie* directly or through the ministers of PL. He is, as has been said, answerable to God for his actions and decisions, having taken upon himself full responsibility for the leadership of his people. It is therefore logical that the Principles should end on his spiritual name, a name trusted, believed in, and invoked by those to whom the Twenty-one Basic Principles represent a practical way of life.

The true test of both Principles and Precepts is, "Do they work? Are they functional? Do they lead the individual toward his highest Self-expression and can they guide mankind toward the Great Peace?"

The answers are strongly affirmative. You not only find them among PL people, you *feel* them. You sense them, and this may well be the most valid criterion. At least, my research convinced me that the true PL follower is bound to surmount the human, natural man as he uses the Twenty-one Basic Principles as the ladder toward his highest good. There is prayer involved here, the mystique of *Oyashikiri*. There is also the strength of fellowship and counsel, and the incomparable satisfaction of doubling the value of life. Living the admonitions daily without display or boasting, the PL follower does efface the ego, develops *Makoto*, and creates a new era for himself through the deepened realization of the truth that *"Oneself is the manifestation of God."*

123

"At that place in life where your talent meets the needs of the world, that is where God wants you to be."

The phrase was perfectly demonstrated. At PL headquarters particularly, everyone seemed to be working toward a common cause, giving the impression that there *is* a special endowment and a specific place in life which combine for a state of harmony and peace.

To me, the personnel in the ranks of PL leadership proved unquestionably through joy and dedication that this was where their talent was needed and this was where God and Oshieoya wanted them to be.

Such a man among these was Dr. Toshio Yasaka, director of BCM (Bureau of Computerized Mission) at Habikino. He and his vocation were inseparably one. Whenever I discussed my questions about PL Principles with him, his answers came both out of his rational reasoning and out of a life which had empirically tested their worth. No one could possibly have been more cooperative or gracious. Even before I arrived at Seichi, this mild-mannered, unassuming scholar had spent long midnight hours transcribing the complicated PL system of opinions and translating them from their involved Japanese terminology into understandable English. He made special copies for me, replete with diagrams and documentation in the dedicated hope that he might properly communicate the metaphysical and cosmological conceptions of a faith dear to his heart and dominating his onward-going research.

A distinguished authority in the fields of psychology, philosophy and semantics, Dr. Yasaka is also a most humble man. Often during my lengthy sessions with him I was humbled by his patience, his quietude, his willingness to go over point after point to make sure the meaning was clear.

Often, too, as I watched him studiously reexamine his notes through his horn-rimmed spectacles, I thought of men in other fields, in every field, in fact, who represent the apperception behind achievements we take for granted. Behind the 747, the aerodynamicist. Behind the computer, the cybernetic expert. Behind the electronic wonders, the scientist cosmic breakthroughs, the creative physicist. Behind the philosophical theories which find their way into popular principles and precepts, the astute and untiring philosopher, a Toshio Yasaka, seeking to absorb the fundamental nature of time and existence in order to comprehend timeless and eternal truth.

I once heard Dr. Yasaka say, "Whenever a man says he is great, he is thinking of the past, and this is not good. A man should continue to express himself. The true Self exists moment by moment and the challenge of PL is ever leading us forward to a more artistic life."

I have no idea how much of the deeper philosophy of PL has filtered through to the rank and file of PL membership any more than I know how much *Christian* doctrine the average Christian has absorbed or how clearly believers in other faiths are conversant with the scholarly studies of their religions. Perhaps this does not matter. One can love without analyzing love, and pray without knowing the anatomy of prayer. One can enjoy food without having a degree in dietetics, or be an artist without a college degree in art. But when we confer with those who are well skilled in both the reach of a subject and the reach of mind, who move easily within the scope of logic and the scope of life, our ground of being becomes more steady and our path more sure.

This was how I felt about Yasaka. Surely his inexhaustible material on *The Principles of Perfect Liberty*, which he subtitled, *A System for an Artistic Life*, will someday find its way into an English edition. Not only PL people but followers of all faiths should have the benefit of his inquiries and study. Important for our purpose are his insights bearing on the conceptual aspects of the Principles and Precepts as these relate to our early reference to the need for recognizing the "Song of Self." This, it seemed to me, was the persistent refrain with which PL was harmonizing total being, and it was this basic truth that Dr. Yasaka clothed with critical analysis and insightful evaluation.

When I spoke earlier of a sense of kinship for Patriarch Miki's life and thought, even before my personal meeting with him, this "Song of Self" was the psychic link of contact. When I met Dr. Yasaka I realized that he, too, had arrived at the same position by way of philosophical inquiry, namely, that the search for meaning *is* the search for Self. Furthermore, he was of the opinion that computer-assisted studies were proving Oshieoya's saying that *Oneself is the manifestation of God.*

"Perfect Liberty," Yasaka explained, "is a movement based on a system of individual self-expressions through an artistic life. Its beginning is the discovery of Self. Its assignment is the effacement of ego. Its challenge is to live the Precepts and Principles. Its ultimate aim is the Great Peace, a time when man will have learned to live harmoniously with himself, his fellowmen and God."

While the philosophical postulates behind the Principles were to be stated in more involved phraseology, Dr. Yasaka made them understandably clear when he said, "The phenomenal universe (the world we know by observation) is grounded in time and space. The noumenal world (the world of Spirit) is limitless in God. One is the world of activity, the other of creativity. The integrative factor is the awareness that life is art."

Having formulated his theory, he suggested that we would grasp the meaning of PL more clearly if we thought in terms of relativity. "The fact that an existence exists," he reflected, "requires and promises the existence of another existence that has a relative function to the former. The

126

function of both suggests an integrated integrity between the two existences. Thus, the universe is One-whole-integrated body operating as One-whole-integrity. The nature of this integrity is God [Kami.] The function of the integrated whole is God-in-action [Kamuwaza.]"

The phenomenal world and the noumenal world, according to PL reasoning, have their specific functions symbolized by an essence relative to their surroundings. The function specific to human beings is the ability to act by a decision of free will. Although a human being is the result of various subfunctions, the center function is always free will. That is why Perfect Liberty both as a movement and an ideal is so important. It insists on an environment in which will may freely function. The will cannot be accounted free if it is enslaved by preconditioning, pre-indoctrination or what the Western world would call the "collective unconscious." A free man is one who approaches life situations as if he were "a sheet of white paper." His characteristic is receptivity. His counsel, divine prompting. His mission, artistic expression. This "whiteness" or open-mindedess requires effort and an exercise of will, and is relative to the degree of power concentrated upon the functioning of the process.

I listened and learned. As I have said, I do not know how much of the cosmological references are part of the average PL follower's knowledge, but the impact of the reasoning touches every life in a mystical way just as the power of Oyashikiri works its wonders even when people do not understand it fully.

Artistic expression, according to Dr. Yasaka, is possible only in cooperation with function of the related existences. This is where Self comes in. To speak of "Self" (or "I") as independent from the surrounding existences has no meaning. Self is a focal, terminal point in the universe. It cannot get outside of the universe and view itself objectively. Self cannot commandeer an out-of-space spacecraft, so to say, and get an objective picture of Self "down here." To say, "I see myself," or "I point out myself," is as preposterous as saying that the eye can see itself. It can only see and sense reflections of itself.

As with "space," so also with "time." In one of his sessions with me, Dr. Yasaka made the point that, "You cannot at this instant write on a blackboard that exists in time twenty minutes from now. You cannot sit at a desk that existed yesterday and then lost its existence. In the same way, Self can only relate to other existences conterminous with the *present*."

I thought again of his words, "Whenever a man says he is great, he is thinking of the past. . . . The true Self exists moment by moment and the challenge of PL is ever leading forward to a more artistic life."

How do these philosophical theories bear upon the Precepts and Principles?

"Take the Precept, *Live radiantly as the Sun*," Yasaka suggested. "Here we have a symbol of a positive power of living and also a unique clarity of expression. Since expression is based upon decision of will and function, the sun-symbol becomes significant. Now we see that decision is inevitably clarification.

"Or consider the precept, *Have true faith in God*. It is inconsistent *not* to have faith in God if one intends to live in the joy of Self-expression. True Self-expression implies correct identification of Self as a manifestation of God.

"Consider the Precept, *Strive for creating mutual happiness*. This relates to universal relativity. Happiness, the subjective joy which is the reflection of Self-expression, is created or produced in both the acting agent and the receiver. The act that imparts happiness to others is such that it will induce the same response in the recipient as in the giver.

"Let us look at the Precept, *Live in perfect unity of mind and matter*. Here we would say that this suggests the co-

128

ordination of the image and the results concretely formed in the world apart from the integrated human being. The degree of achievement of this unity represents the degree of happiness or joy of Self-expression."

Self, I learned through my seminars with Dr. Yasaka, has the ability to relate the decided will to existences and to integrate the specific functions of the existences in the form the will has imaged. The depth of the function depends upon the degree or strength of the decision of the will and the functions. He referred to this as "output." The ability of the Self to relate to the environmental existences when the will is undecided, this he labeled as "input." In the case of input, the less decided the will, the more precise the understanding realized inside the integrated body.

It should be explained here that these meetings with Toshio Yasaka were not as heavy or "heady" as my report on them may imply. We met in a small classroom adjoining his office in Assembly Hall No. 2 at hours which he cordially arranged to suit my schedule whether early morning or late at night. Rarely were we without the traditional "tea break," served by several Japanese girls, students, who seemed to sense just when we needed a pick-up of tea and cakes. Then our conversation drifted into subjects far afield from the strict philosophy of PL, but not for long! Soon my instructor was back to his cherished topics: the Precepts, the Principles, Oshieoya, the influence of PL, the wonders of *Kami* and *Kamuwaza*, the meaning of Self.

"Self is the subjective function," he continually sought to make clear, "and is not able to place itself in the position of object. Self is the most exalted existence in the universe. Even the work of *Kami* (spiritual dynamism) is under its recognition. Because Self recognizes *Kami*, *Kami* exists. Self is *Kami* manifested. The only identity of Self exists in the process of expression. One should, therefore, identify oneself in *all* expressions. Expressions are possible only with the function of the related existences. So, once again, Self

129

independent of the surrounding existences has no meaning. The idea of exclusiveness merely disturbs the effect of Self-expression in such a way as to cause a person to be obsessed with 'I' and place his identity in an exaggerated position."

So spoke PL's interpreter, Toshio Yasaka, a man who, in his mid-forties, felt he was just now beginning to discover the path of ever-unfolding truth, truth which he put into such scholarly categories as *"Neighborhoods in Subject-Object Relationships," "Concepts," "Desire Motives,"* analogues on the structure of the universe and the nature of Self. Most of all, he was dedicated to the exciting task of testing Principle and Precept through the BCM approach.

But what impressed me most was Dr. Yasaka's effacement of ego and his quietude of life. This reflection of the teachings in life, I kept telling myself, is PL's strength. It lies in the people. It is demonstrated in Oshieoya. PL shapes and forms and changes life, perfecting it. PL itself as a *movement* expresses the truth that "Life is Art." And though Yasaka walked, as philosophers so often do, in realms of thought beyond the average man, he never lost touch with those who shared his quest.

"Whenever a man says he is great, he is thinking of the past, and this is not good. A man should continue to express himself. The true Self exists moment by moment and the challenge of Perfect Liberty is ever leading us forward to a more artistic life."

■ 4 ■

The "Computerized Mission" involves a distinguished staff of scholars headed by Oshieoya. The assignment he has entrusted to himself and his co-workers is laboratory research in the fields of health and healing, studies in man's relationship with himself and his environment, and practical application of the Precepts and Principles as these relate to PL people and to the world at large.

The computerized laboratory itself is of imposing proportions. The instrumentation, housed in Assembly Hall No. 2 on the fourth floor, reminded me of the data processing equipment one finds in highly sophisticated industrial research centers. When I was shown through these batteries of electronic wonders, I had to keep reminding myself that this was indeed a headquarters of *spiritual* development, a far and daring step ahead of most institutionalized religious enterprises no matter where they are located.

Where is there another "church headquarters" that evaluates the influence of Spirit scientifically, that analyzes, tests and appraises the movement of the "divine"? I felt I was in a kind of spiritual seismographic lab where mysterious mechanisms were recording the tremors of God in the life of man! There was absorbing fascination here and a graphic closing of the gap between science and religion unmatched, as I have said, anywhere in the world. Certainly the staff members never lose sight of this fact. They know that the coordinating factor is God-in-the-life-of-man.

"The PL Hospital," says PL publications, "aims at a firm establishment of PL medicine by proving one of our religious doctrines that says illness is the revelation of God, and a man becomes ill when he violates divine law. Both the doctors and the patients pray to God for mercy prior to the medical treatment, and also in the waiting room the patients pray and worship in front of an altar. Due to mutual trust between doctors and patients, all of whom are believers of the same religion, the cures are most effective."

Small wonder that one man remarked to me, "If I get sick, may I, by the grace of God, be close to Hoshokai Hospital!" There is no doubt in my mind that this is the consensus of PL people generally who because of their membership in PL have ready access to the services here available. The distinguished medical staff include such men as pathologist Shigeru Matsuoka of Nagasaki Medical College, Dr. Torijiro Ikemi of Kyushu University's Medical School,

131

and pediatrician K. Murakami, who is also director of the hospital.

In my meeting with one of the most active members of the medical faculty, Dr. Keijiro Kiyoshima, I was again struck by the vitality and devotion of PL personnel. This young, dynamic, amazingly quick-thinking physician more than conformed to my point of view about those who feel they are in the right place at the right time. Dr. Kiyoshima, a man with highly specialized medical training that includes three years of study in the United States, is a surgeon specializing in stomach disorders, yet one who, as most members of the PL hospital staff, is also a qualified PL minister.

No doubt this is the direction that the faiths of mankind generally will take in the years ahead, an interrelationship between medicine and religion. As in the early dawning of civilization the priest was the physician, and the physician, priest, this concept has come full circle at PL headquarters, but with an ultra-modern touch. Here we find physical and emotional examinations, computer-assisted, and actual scientific testing of the use of prayer (*Oyashikiri*) and divine instruction (*Mioshie*). What could be more exciting or more prophetic as the onward march of faith seeks to effect at long last "inner peace" so that a new course may be charted to the Great Peace in all the world!

Now, obviously, the union of "spiritual healing" and allopathic therapies has long been part of the trend in America. Certain denominations such as the Adventists particularly and other Christian faiths have consistently made the treatment of disease paramount in their missionary outreach. Medical missions are historic facts and there is a universal trend to narrow the breach between religion and science. But in view of this and by these standards, PL becomes all the more unique.

Here at PL Hospital medical doctors, psychiatrists, dental specialists and therapists demonstrate an amazing spiritual attunement among themselves and with their patients.

Here Oshieoya plays a direct role in the healing process through his in-depth analysis and his personalized "prescriptions" of *Mioshie*. Even more, here the Computerized Mission's interdisciplinary research, creative studies about the nature of human life, unite with philosophical concepts aiming at new breakthroughs in *preventive* medicine. Keep the well from getting sick! Learn to live in keeping with natural law! Use your divine warnings as steppingstones to health! This is what PL is driving at.

Dr. Kiyoshima's enthusiasm for the process by which PL institutes its diagnoses and effects its cures was more than understandable. He explained that PL now has nearly a million pieces of accumulated data relating to personalized reports on all kinds of *Mishirases*.

"This treasury of material," he made clear, "includes case histories of diseases, accidents, mental disturbances, social conflicts. These are analyzed on the basis of medical science and in the light of subjective reasoning and are then related to the field of preventive medicine."

Deduction assists in statistically discovering from this vast data the causative elements of mental behavior, and, based on the detected factors, it is possible to form a "mental structure" that may be considered as the cause of the problem. The next step is the transformation of the mental behavior into the subjective view of the person who has the problem. This is referred to as the "living structure" since it is a description of the way in which the person looks at his environment. Since the understanding of the environment is the mirror of subjective insight, the patient's mental habit is reflected in the phenomenon as he understands it. A questionnaire is employed with questions bearing upon the problem or problems of the patient and this has been checked by Oshieoya as to its relative effectiveness.

At this point it is necessary to review Oshieoya's conclusions about the nature of the individual, an insight which I have earlier referred to as being both psychic and extrasensory as well as the result of uncommon spiritual awareness. Oshieoya has in mind an image of what he calls the "ideal person" to which he has given the identification *Hito*, but *Hito* in a larger sense than merely "Man." *Hito* in the Patriarch's frame of reference is that hypothetical or actual individual who fulfills all the requirements of the Twenty-one Precepts, who has effaced the ego, and who is faithful to the Twenty-one Basic Principles. *Hito*, the new man, has the ability to create a new truth in the universe because of his intensified human power. Truth or universal law, as produced by *Hito*, is comparable to the mystical force inherent in *Oyashikiri*. Oshieoya calls this force the "Originating Power." *Hito*, therefore, is one who can grasp the center of facts through direct, intuitive capability which is the very essence of *Mioshie*.

To further understand this sequence leading to the "ideal person" and to realize how the restoration and healing of individuals at Hoshokai conform to PL belief, it is well to remember that PL people believe that the enlightenment of *Hito* is embodied in Oshieoya. The PL movement may be said to be the "living art" of Oshieoya personified in his people. Oshieoya originates the power of *Oyashikiri*, gives *Mioshie*, and transmits the power of *Mioshie* through the ministers who serve in his name.

These facts must be borne in mind when judging the value and function of the questionnaire. It is more than a data sheet on the psychological and emotional state of a patient, it is a fact sheet weighed in the light of *Hito*. On this basis advice is given and with the help of the computer, *Mioshie* is created, based both on Oshieoya's present evaluation and on the vast records of *Mishirase* and *Mioshie* tucked away in the electronic memory banks and instantly available for clinical use. When the development of this method is completely achieved, as it will be shortly, it will be possible, by direct on-line service from all over the world, to serve the millions of PL affiliates no less than non-PL people who are caught in divine warnings or who need the help that only Hoshokai Hospital can provide. PL is already handling some five hundred *Mishirases* each day, sent in by ministers at PL centers who, on behalf of their people, seek the charting of a proper *Mioshie*.

Dr. Kiyoshima is of the opinion that divine warnings have a constructive purpose: they provide an opportunity to correct minor errors before major errors arise which may lead to more injurious effects. He cited graphic and practical illustrations out of recent case histories. For example, consider the well-known tendency toward haste or impatience. Here is a housewife who insists on watching the kettle, picking it up, urging the water to boil, constantly taking off the lid, complaining about the small flame, not realizing she is at fault, unaware that when something happens in the mind there is a physiological reaction as its equivalent.

Here is a man continually showing his impatience with a copying machine by pulling out the paper prematurely and contemplating the terrible qualities of the instrument without realizing that his action can lead to a larger psychosis. Hurrying people dial the telephone badly, often write illegibly and speak incoherently. Innumerable tests have shown that anger, jealousy, envy, covetousness have damaging toxic effects. Obviously if these tendencies are not curbed *Mishirases* will follow

Dr. Kiyoshima told about an auto accident precipitated because a man was driving overly fast to his work. He had been late the day before and had been upbraided by his boss. As he drove this time he thought, "I won't be late again. I must go as fast as possible." He had already had symptoms of *Mishirase* such as sweating and nervous tension which should have alerted him to the error of his ways. His haste also caused a narrowed vision but, unheeding these warnings, he stepped on the gas and collided with another car at an intersection. Even in cases as obvious as these, the Computerized Mission should be able to ferret out the probabilities and prevent the ultimate consequences.

"If a person is stubborn and knows it," says Dr. Kiyoshima, "this is conscious and will not cause *Mishirase*. But the computer should embody the technique to detect if the subject is stubborn and *unconscious* of the fact. The questionnaire will assist in the programming by asking such questions as, 'Do you have anyone who does not agree with you? Are there people who have difficulty in seeing your point of view? Do you consider yourself a person of strong sense of duty and obligation? Do you confront situations that force you to conclude that your opinions and ideas are not easily acceptable to others?' So the questionnaire becomes a mirror. And the *Mioshie* will deal with the situation, turn the *Mishirase* into a blessing, and restore the person whole and well to a rededication of the Principles and Precepts."

The PL life, Dr. Kiyoshima believes, is the balanced life, and the balanced life has health and happiness as its natural concomitant. *Oyashikiri*, he feels, is of utmost help to him in his ability as a surgeon. *Oyashikiri* helps him in his work, it helps the patients in their attitude, it is effective in assuring more speedy recovery after surgery.

As Dr. Kiyoshima views the PL process, the continuity runs like this: the Twenty-one Precepts and Principles represent the guidelines for a balanced life. By a process of deduction the causative factors of mental and physical conditioning are determined. The system of analyzing the emotions involves inductive reasoning, using the scientifically programmed da a of *Mishirases* and *Mioshies*. The computer-assisted medical examination is the most thorough to be found anywhere. In fact, Hoshokai Hospital is architecturally designed for the ultimate in efficiency and with the patient's total well-being in mind. The corrective processes are hastened through BCM and the religious-scientific approach assures each patient of the utmost in spiritual as well as physical cures.

Dr. Kiyoshima believes, as does every member of the hospital staff, that "Man can live a worthy life only when he consciously communes with God." When mankind truly lives the Precepts and obeys the Basic Principles, only then will it be possible to realize the advent of the "*Hito*" man so graphically personified in Patriarch Miki.

How prophetic this all sounded and how strangely it all fit together! After all, there *are* Twenty-one Precepts and Twenty-one Basic Principles and there *is*, everywhere in the world, the prediction of the coming of a new type twenty-first century man, a new creature governed by inner creativity and uniting the phenomenal and the noumenal worlds!

It seemed more than mere coincidence that Oshieoya should be speaking of his view of this new man and it was surely more than chance that PL research and PL innovations were going forward on such a magnificent scale at Habikino. What was really happening here? How was the phenomenal impact of this new religion to be explained.

It occurred to me that in a world where self-reliance is continually being down-graded, where self-awareness is constantly being sapped, where ego-inflation has become a disastrous way of life—in a world where the human being is often less than human—it is at this very point that PL is setting a new scene and creating its new life-style, seeking to convince the world that the *new man* is already here. He is each man's own and deepest still-to-be-realized Self!

And PL in its Precepts and Principles has the working plan for that realization.

Chapter Eight

THE POWER OF PERFECT LIBERTY

■ 1 ■

DURING MY STAY at PL headquarters I frequently heard and occasionally saw in print the words, "Peace Man." At first they struck me as a Japanese-ism of the kind that frequently shows up in translation, but the term grew on me. There are peace makers and there are peace *men*. There are those who negotiate and plan for peace and there are those who live it, and through the living of it create the conditions by which peace can be secured. Without the peace man the peace *makers* would hardly have a chance. PL believes that in the new dispensation, peace makers must first of all be "Peace Men." That is, the new man must demonstrate peace within himself, not in an isolated fashion, but in his total involvement with life.

The "Great Peace" according to PL, will emerge from such a state of being, not from negotiations. It will be born out of spirit rather than forged out of diplomacy around a bargaining table. Idealistically the Great Peace will be an extension of peace in the heart. Inevitably it will be recognized as a work of art, the creative product of the new man, the "Peace Man," the *Hito-man* in the new sense given it by Oshieoya.

Here, then, is a bold idea, a creative dimension in humanity's long search for meaning in life and an end to war. When the art of living becomes more heroic than the diabolic genius of destruction and death, peace becomes inevitable. When the peace man becomes not only the symbol but the reality of all that is honorable and constructive, a new value is placed on life. PL is saying that this hour of decision has come and its call has gone out for a worldwide mobilization of those who will catch the vision.

Many have already caught it.

I had often been plagued by a feeling of aloneness whenever I contemplated my role and my aspiration as an advocate of peace. I was convinced that demonstrations against war were as paradoxical as war itself and I had often seen rallies for peace flare into violence. Nonresistance frequently triggered resistance and bloodshed. Political loyalties could be dangerously misplaced, and even religious crusades for peace implied the virtue of one party's God over another's. I had felt the frustration of investing my persuasions in "just causes for peace" when these inevitably resulted in polemics against war or in prolonged dissension among the contenders.

Patriarch Miki was right. The world needs a new breed of people who have the courage to look upon themselves as equal to the task of building a better world and of structuring the Great Peace. If we are made in the image of God, or if the image of God is in us, we should begin putting the emphasis upon the highest side of our nature. The *Hito-man!* Life to him will be total living!

It occurred to me that we in the Western world have a

deep-seated feeling that in order to realize this "highest side" of our nature, we must shun "materialism." Many of us have been brought up on the gospel of duality. There is always God's side and man's side. PL's approach is monistic. It calls for harmonization of the two forces, spirituality and materialism, because it sees them as one. And in this sense of oneness lies much of the power of Perfect Liberty.

We are human *and* divine and no one has yet been able to tell where one leaves off and the other begins. PL's interlocking signal is always, "Life is Art!" Patriarch Miki's counsel is clear, "PL is a pilot to your own utopia!"

For those who went with this kind of hope to Seichi, as I did, things began to happen. They recognized immediately that there were others stirred by this same apocalyptic dream, this unique and heartfelt knowing that *the Hito-man is a balanced man*, building toward a balanced world in a new century.

This aspiration has taken root in the awareness of true devotion, the *Misasage* of Perfect Liberty. Its members demonstrate it wherever they live, and that is everywhere in Japan, in every major city, in villages, and in the countryside. PL's membership reaches into North and South America, into Europe, it is, in fact, a leaven in the global society of the world. For them, true identity is world identity, and inner peace is the inevitable path to universal brotherhood.

Keyed to psychological pursuits no less than to religious and philosophical disciplines, PL makes no distinction between East or West, spirituality or materialism, Christian or non-Christian. Ever since 1946 when Tokuchika Miki designated this new movement "Perfect Liberty" he pledged himself toward meeting the challenge of a world in transition and in shaping a blueprint for the social renaissance hoped for in our tomorrows. Whether world situations make the man or whether the man is called to make the situation, the leader behind the PL movement had been so prophetic in the past that when he now predicted the coming of the new man in a new century, he was justified in being taken seriously.

On that day in 1946 when Miki was questioned by many of his followers on the advisability of using an English title for the extension of *Hito-no-Michi*, he replied,

"The teachings of PL are universal and should not remain the exclusive religion of a limited number of Japanese. It is my solemn duty and responsibility to propagate the PL doctrine throughout the globe. So, words from a language (English) that I consider the most universal are used to signify my conviction that what I teach is for the benefit of all mankind."

That is how it happened. That is how a new life style came into prominence, and the years have proved Miki's pronouncement unmistakably prophetic. New generations, convinced that a new age was imminent, confident that war is no longer relevant, their pleas unheeded by governments, disenfranchised by ancient dogmas out of which the meaning had gone, had been on a search for a man and a movement which would serve as a rallying point for the consolidation of their aspirations. To them, Perfect Liberty offered philosophical and physical training, a new expression of intercultural comaraderie and impressive challenges and techniques to live by.

The timing of PL was perfect.

■ 2 ■

A graphic example of how the power of PL was being released was impressed upon me by a young American student who during his visit to EXPO 70 joined a group of two hundred young people who attended a Fine Arts Seminar at Seichi. The emphasis was on creativity in the fields of ceramics, textile painting, sculpture, poetry, and also participation in the deeper symbolism of the tea ceremony.

All of this was interesting, but what caught the student's attention was the PL way of life. It was in such sharp contrast to his previous concerns and so far removed from his frustrations, that he was deeply impressed.

"I had never been in such surroundings before," he told me, "or met people who had such an outlook on life. After spending a day with them, I walked away by myself to think the whole thing through. Why did I have a different feeling about the world and myself when I was with these people of PL?"

The real world to him had been the unrest and violence on college campuses, the war, racial conflicts, his own struggle for a sense of values. These concerns had been continually on his mind, but now he was feeling a thrill of unity and oneness with PL people. Why, he wondered, were his deep-seated concerns suddenly absorbed by the apparent simplicity of it all?

He toured the Peace Tower with other young people. This towering memorial has become one of Japan's most inspiring attractions both from the standpoint of art and its inherent symbolism. While it commemorates the "war dead" of all nations and of all times, it immortalises the living who perpetuate humanity's dream for a warless world. P-E-A-C-E, as referred to in the Tower, is an acronym:

P—Pray for peace.
E—Enshrine peace in your heart.
A—Aspire to peace through Perfect Liberty.
C—Commemorate those who sacrificed for peace.
E—Enlighten others toward universal peace.

The Peace Tower awakened more than symbolism in the American student. He remembered having read an editorial in his hometown paper which contended that the vast masses in Southeast Asia would rather weave rugs and make baskets than be trained to kill. Most people, if they had a choice, would prefer love over hate, peace over war, truth

143

over falsehood, beauty over ugliness. So said the news story and he thought of it as he participated in the Fine Arts Seminar. Wasn't this what PL was driving at in its insistence that "Life Is Art?"

He was a Christian and had been a leader in his church's youth fellowship, but he had heard nothing in PL that conflicted with his Christian way of thinking. In fact, PL was putting a *Christian* responsibility upon him to live his beliefs. The PL seminar people gave the impression that in the sheer pleasure of being and doing, problems that beset the world could be overcome, challenges could be met and solved, and questions could be answered through a new sense of direction in life. The artist somehow became a child of innocence and ecstasy, and the child became a man—of art.

The student was quite right. In its artistic approach to life, PL does reflect ethical Christianity in action. Its Art Seminars are a way of saying, "Whosoever does not receive the kingdom of God like a little child shall not enter therein." Fellowship at Seichi is a graphic demonstration of how, for a while, at least, people can have all things in common. At the same time, in its demand for commitment, in its insistence that men must rise above humanness into a "new generation," PL has the salvation not only of the individual but of humanity at heart.

If this is reality, this is power, and all the warfields and slaughter and body counts and violence are made incomprehensible in the prophetic concept of the artistry of life.

■ 3 ■

The global outreach of the power of PL is effectively centered in PLAI (Perfect Liberty Association International).

This organizational arm of the movement is so modern

144

that when I joined it I was not surprised to find my membership credential in the form of a high-style "credit card" issued through the American offices of Perfect Liberty at 700 South Adams Street, Glendale, California. Comparing favorably in design with our commercial credit cards, the embossed PL warranty is different and distinctive in at least one respect. On its reverse side are five compelling affirmations which I have yet to see on any commercial credit card anywhere:

1. I live for the joy of an artistic life.
2. I pray for the happiness of others.
3. I live with true effort and sincerity.
4. I maintain the highest dignity and honor.
5. I strive for great peace of the world.

This is PL in action in the business, professional and social world. The PLAI card assured me that I was now a link in an expanding chain of peace and understanding around the globe, and who has not felt the need and promise of something along this line? Who has not thought about an international, intercultural affiliation with a "credit card" to obtain not material goods, but goodwill and fellowship.

The plan is for each PL church to be a cultural and fine arts center, with PLAI membership providing participation in such activities as golf, ceramics, poetry, flower arranging, instruction in Japanese cuisine, textile painting, calligraphy and other areas. Eventually Western membership will also include, as it does already in Japan, medical services and healing therapies.

Total health for the total person may prove to be the most powerful factor in the PLAI program. This applies not only to health care as related to pathological and accidental situations, but to the balance and function of the nervous system in its relationship to health and healing.

Patriarch Miki has a strong point in his insistence that, "Man has emotions, and the change of emotions affects his life. One's emotional life must be controlled first of all.

Unbalanced conditions of emotions result in unforeseen accidents, physical illness, family troubles, and general unhappiness. PL, through PLAI, is designed to effectively and scientifically prove that *man can control his destiny by the proper control of emotions.*"

How thoroughly and with what sophisticated modern methods PLAI deals with this field of "overall health control" is impressed upon everyone who visits the Medical Center in the new PLAI Building in Tokyo. Here research in the relationship of psyche and soma is being developed on an unparalleled scale. Medical specialists, skilled psychoanalysts, precise instrumentation combine to serve the health of people in relation to their mental, behavioral and physical surroundings, catching any indisposition in time to prevent illness or to control and cure the sickness once it has been incurred.

"PLAI watches your health even when you forget to take care of yourself," is the PL promise. "You are kept informed every month. You receive a medical check-up twice a year. Diagnosis is made accurate by computers to handle the data quickly and perfectly. It takes only three hours to complete your thorough medical examination."

Located in the PLAI Building is PL's efficient "Management Consulting Center." Here your business, your industries, your commercial enterprises receive their diagnostic service. Expert managerial consultants provide analysis and advice, conduct seminars, and hold self-improvement sessions for business executives.

"PLAI," says Patriarch Miki, "seeks to create men of great peace and ability in an artistic world by promoting mutual happiness through the harmonious self-expression of individuality and by contributing to society improved means of understanding and cooperation among all people."

This is PL's teleological approach to the new age. This is the ethos of the new man, made whole by philosophy, kept physically alert and well by a discipline, harmonized with himself and his environment by the knowledge that he bears within himself the destiny and hope of a truly new view of the world.

If idealism of this kind, set within the framework of total peace, seems unrealistic, if there are those who think peace itself is an idyllic dream, there are millions of people of every race and creed who, as has been said, are thoroughly convinced of the inevitable coming of the *"Hito-man."*

■ 4 ■

How are these new individuals for a new century mobilized? The plan, of course, is to join PLAI. The idea is to affiliate with a PL center. But the Patriarch makes it clear that PL as a philosophical approach to life can be lived by anyone and is being lived by many who are not specifically members of a PL church.

Missionary activity, however, is growing, and all members of PL are reaching out for people interested in investigating the key which PL holds to the new age. The power of *Makoto* has an attractive appeal. Study courses in how to realize *Makoto* are being prepared and many types of social activities are being promoted. Pilgrimages to *Habikino* and the *Rensei* training are part of the advanced missionary effort. The idea is to influence and convert the individual to PL Principles and Precepts and then stimulate his spiritual action on a larger than personal front.

I met a woman who became a follower of PL because she heard about a class in flower arrangement (*Ikebana*) in a neighborhood PL church. All she knew about this religion was that the minister was Japanese and that more and more people were beginning to attend the services. She was Caucasian, a drop-out Protestant, and had learned to live quite well without the benefit of an institutionalized faith. Interested in flowers, however, she was attracted by the course of study in this particular art.

On her first visit she saw the young Japanese *Ikebana*

teacher demonstrate how a single thistle flower could be displayed so attractively it seemed to have caught a bit of magic. Describing this to me, the woman said with enthusiasm, "Did you know that by a simple touch, if you know the technique, you can change the whole artistic plan of anything?"

She had caught the deeper implications. There is not only *Ikebana* of flowers, there is an *Ikebana* of total being. Flower arranging imparted to her a new sense of reliability and confidence in herself. *Ikebana*, creative in an outer way, proceeded to change her life from within. Flower artistry, which originated in Oriental temples, was here transferred to the temple of life.

PL taught this woman something about God without talking about God and transmitted religious truth without preaching about religion. As one arranges flowers with one's mind in tune with nature, so life can be tuned to goodness and beauty. She also learned that as flowers respond to art, so the individual responds to all that is suggested to him and that he suggests to himself. In exactly the same way, the universe responds to the qualities of all its parts, both to the elements and all mankind.

This kind of reasoning brought this woman by a form of logic, straight into the teachings of PL. *Ikebana* opened the door to Perfect Liberty's major Precept, "Life Is Art," and prepared her potentially for fellowship in a new fraternity of spirit.

What PL is aiming at through a thistle flower or a golf game or a piece of ceramic art or by way of a creative poem or a prayer before the *Omitama* is the conviction that the power upon which a nation rises or falls, lives or dies, lies in the art of the individual.

Every culture is the result of its spiritual art form, says PL. What we express at the deepest core of our being shapes our society. How we conduct ourselves as individuals and as a nation in our moments of stress, tension, confrontation and challenge creates our basic image.

Our relationship to the universe, the cosmic awareness within ourselves dictates our national character. What we hold as our basic sense of values determines our impression upon the world at large.

If this total overview of life can be made to work, if individuals can be persuaded to find harmony within themselves and with others by means of art and creativity and a thorough-going joy of living, PLAI is bound to succeed, and Patriarch Miki will one day be hailed as the architect of the Great Peace.

The Power of PL!

LIFE IS ART—ALL IS A MIRROR—COMPREHEND WHAT IS MOST ESSENTIAL—LIVE IN PERFECT UNITY OF MIND AND MATTER—MAN'S LIFE IS A SUCCESSION OF SELF-EXPRESSIONS—AT EVERY MOMENT MAN STANDS AT THE CROSSROADS OF GOOD AND EVIL.

To confront a war-weary world and a polluted earth with uncritical Precepts of this kind—twenty-one of them—is sufficiently incredible to fire the imagination of those who have been languishing for a breakthrough of a new and revolutionary ideological ideal. The challenge is just daring enough to enlist the loyalties of energetic thinking people. Just enough to make us wonder whether in a world where miracles of outer space have captured universal attention, there might be something here that promises similar sensational discoveries in an adventure inward.

There are those among us who have never been convinced that either we or our planet have actually lost our way, and we have secretly felt that the road back or forward to sanity and peace would be clearly marked with spiritually illuminated signs.

Wherever my sharing of religions' beliefs has taken me —to campuses, traditional churches, sensitivity sessions—

the test of contemporary religion has consistently been: "What does it do to *me?*" The corollary was clearly, "What does it do to *others?*" The implication was obviously, "What would the world be like if everyone followed this particular religion's teachings?"

This marketplace appraisal of modern faith asks to what extent a religion inspires society to be more compassionate, moral, creative. An evaluation of religion is no longer based on theological, historic or denominational premises. As for apocalyptic prophecies or promises involving heaven and salvation, even the evangelists have mellowed on their former irrevocable verdicts as to who will or will not be saved.

The stark fact of human survival in this life has overshadowed the once impassioned anxiety for the life-to-come. Youth of the world, looking for their own kind of religion, know that one of its tenets will have to be not only the making of peace with men, but with nature. Another tenet will be an insistence that religion dare no longer be kept far afield from life, separate from the joy of living or removed from the legitimate things to which people devote most of their time in life. Golf may not be a spiritual act but why should it not have spiritual implications? *Ikebana* may not be a sacrament, but why can it not have sacramental overtones? Why should man's transactions with man in the business world not represent a certain type of communion?

This is what PL is driving at. It has been saying for a long time that when work becomes worship, religion is truly lived, and where art is expressed in total life, God is truly recognized.

I once asked the Rev. Jiro Yano, Administrator of Education at *Seichi*, at what point this program for the development of the new man actually begins.

"Before birth," he said. "Children are the mirror of their parents. The nature of a child is formed by the thoughts and actions of its parents before it is born. Parents are the first teachers. Children imitate. The child's first expression should be respected by the parents. The child has a dignity of personality which *must* be respected. It should not be warped by the parents' selfishness or, as Oshieoya so often warns, 'doting on their children,' or on the superimposition of the parents' will. If we learn to respect children's God-given nature, then they will grow up as resourceful and useful citizens of society. Discipline is a part of art, or art is a discipline."

What about "mother love," the abundance of which we so strongly emphasize in the western world?

"Affection," said Administration Yano, "must be objective. A calm, reasoned affection is best. It should not be a blind, exciting, concerned mother love which can, in fact, spoil the child. Patriarch Miki has wisely pointed out that a mother looking continually at her child in the cradle, doting on her child, is exalting her own ego.

"When we read the Precepts aright and live them, we already have a sound basis for bringing up our children. The responsibility, then, is upon us. Life always wishes to resolve itself into a matter of balance. Respect the child's volition, individuality and involuntary actions, and then quietly and wisely exercise discipline.

"Sometimes, I grant you, it is difficult to distinguish between a child's true expression and its selfish desire which is a mirror of the parents' ego. We may not be infallible in making the best possible moves when we have decisions to make or lives to guide, but if we weigh our decisions against the Precepts, particularly the one that says *Life Is Art*, and if we keep in mind the qualities of the new man, we have a sound and workable basis for honest judgment."

Sometimes a hint of the appearance of the "new man" appears in the news. Such was the case during the dramatic skyjacking of a Japanese airliner on its April 10, 1970, flight from Tokyo to Fukuoka. The three-engine jet had just gotten its 122 passengers airborne when nine young men leaped from their seats brandishing daggers and *samurai* swords. Holding a sword at the captain's throat, they ordered him to fly to Pyongyang, North Korea. They called themselves the "Red Army."

For three days the story of this nerve-racking flight held the concern and eerie fascination of an apprehensive world. Part of the fantastic saga was even televised, the refueling at Fukuoka, the ruse on the part of the crew to land the plane at Kimpo airport in South Korea in a vain attempt to persuade the skyjackers that they were actually at Pyongyang, the threats, the terrorizing, the graphic impasse, all heightened this weird, cloak-and-dagger spectacular.

The climax came when a Japanese negotiator, Vice President of Transport, Shinjiro Yamamura, offered himself as hostage in place of the passengers and guaranteed with his life the flight to Pyongyang. The skyjackers allowed the passengers to disembark. The 39-year-old Yamamura boarded the plane alone in a significant act of courage and a new approach to the war of nerves in the sky.

When the crew and Yamamura brought the plane safely back from North Korea, an intimate detail in the drama was quietly noted. The wife of Shinjiro Yamamura, it was reported, was a devoted member of PL. She had done *Oyashikiri* throughout her husband's bold adventure and she believed that through the power of prayer, what might have been a tragic affair became a *Mishirase* of the kind that caused PL to cite the action of Mr. Yamamura as a creative act, a work of art, the courage and character of the new man.

Such recognition is understandable when we remember PL's belief that the true art on which a nation rises or falls, lives or dies, is the *art of the individual life*. PL considers every culture a reflection of its spiritual art form. What the individual believes at the deepest core of his being shapes society. How we conduct ourselves as individuals in times of stress no less than in times of prosperity and peace fashions our national image. Our relationship to the universe, the cosmic consciousness within us defines our social character. What each man holds as his basic sense of values ultimately determines the cultural quality of his cooperative life.

That is why the action of a man like Shinjiro Yamamura was so significant. Himself a PL member, as I learned later, he demonstrated those qualities of faith and courage which are the credentials of all religions, Christian and non-Christian, and the hope and aim of all philosophies.

Life is Art within the present moment. We express our highest state of spirituality by using contemporary challenges as the stuff to make our lives artistic and worthwhile. Religon shapes the individual. Individuals shape the world. So says PL.

■ 6 ■

Speaking of spiritual power and the spiritual man, in my talks with PL leaders, there was never any doubt in my mind about their respect and admiration for Christian teachings. But whenever I put theological questions to them, inquiries having to do with the nature of sin, salvation, life after death, Christ's "second coming," and the like, the answer was invariably a patient smile. Such an enigmatic response said more than words. It conveyed the impression of "One world at a time, please." It reflected the Buddha's famous comment, "I have not answered all the questions about this world, how can I tell you about the next?" It bore on Jesus' famous rhetoric, "Sufficient unto the day is the evil thereof." It was Oshieoya saying, "What more is needed than living the truth that *Life Is Art?*"

I once asked Rev. Koreaki Yano whether he believed heaven to be a location or a state of consciousness. He replied, "Who but God knows about these things? The thing we know is that we are living *now*. We know there are things to be done and that we are here to build a better world. That is a big enough assignment. Life is given by God so that we may create a better life for all."

"Do you believe we will live again?"

"There are many ways of living on after the experience we call death," he said. "We live on in our children. We live on in the friends and people we have influenced. There are impressions we have made that lie dormant for a time, as seeds do, before they begin to grow and bear fruit. Perhaps there is another world, a spirit world, or a world that we cannot even imagine. But there is so much to do in life on earth that we should concentrate on this, knowing that the next life will take care of itself."

"But," I argued, "shouldn't we prepare ourselves for the life to come and know something about it? After all, when we take a trip to a foreign country we read books about it and prepare ourselves for what we may rightly expect."

"Did you know anything about *this* life before you were born?" he asked. "Life is life. No matter how you study or read about foreign countries, there are always surprises in store when you get there. One person writes about a country as he saw it and another as it seemed to him. Think how difficult it must be to write about countries you have *not* seen! The best preparation for the future life is to live one's best in this life."

When I asked for PL's views about "original sin" and the need for redemption, the answer again was a patient smile.

"PL does not relate to the concept of sin in a Western sense," Koreaki Yano mused. "Being saved and redemption and salvation are, I think, Christian terms. I would say that original sin, or original blessings, for that matter, are things we inherit from our ancestors. Through many generations our life has been formed and a great deal of our character was already established or conditioned before we were born. I am here because I have ancestors. Parents express through us in a constructive or destructive way. If I in-

154

herit the virtues of my ancestors there is also a possibility of inheriting their vices. I must remember this in relation to my own children. I carry the responsibility both of my ancestors and my children. I am a deciding factor in how my children will turn out.

"Oshieoya explains that the 'mirror' consists of various "paths" or reflections, all of which teach us something of the children's behavior and also of our own ancestry. When we find something wrong in the condition of our children, we should remember that the mirror reproduces the character of grandparents, great grandparents and so on. When we have a matter to resolve in the child's character and are worried about his future, it is best to receive *Mioshie*, because the trouble is a *Mishirase*. *Mioshie* will clearly reveal the errors of both parents and ancestors as well as the child."

While there is a good deal of Shinto and Buddhist philosophy in all this, the "mirror" of PL thought also reflects the introspection of modern psychology and provides a coherent philosophical view for those who relate the expositions of Patriarch Miki to life. This, too, is PL's power. It is extremely sensitized and coherent to modern thought and allows for freedom to meet practical innovations while maintaining its roots in ancient truths. It would by no means agree that God was more real, closer to men, or more revelatory in the distant past than He is now. *Every age is God's age.* Every change is another chapter in the exciting book of revelation.

If the past *is* indispensable to us, says PL, then let us by all means control it and not let it control us. In this respect the Precepts represent, as we have said, a sort of conscience, of the kind that doctrinal injunctions are striving for in other faiths. Any attempt to make the speculative dogmatic, however, or any specious argument that seeks to make suppositions infallible receive the response of what I have called the "patient smile."

Religions which insist on remaining changeless seem to

PL interpreters like artists limited to working in one medium only. When the material for that medium runs out, the artist ceases to be artistic. The versatile artist, however, will experiment with new mediums. PL says, "That which is around us is waiting to be created," and implores its followers to see the hand of God in a changing world. It believes that if a man reacts in the same way to a given situation year after year, then it is the situation and not the man that governs the action.

When the American college student mentioned the conflict he felt between his idealism and reality and of the closing of the gap that came to him at PL headquarters, the reason for his feeling was clear. PL insists on the recognition of one's *Self* as the most important and most interesting phenomenon in the world, and not even the overpowering influence of world situations should rob one of this fact.

"I do not regard Self as my master," a PL convert wrote me. "Self is what I *am*, and unless I mirror Self in this true way, I have a distorted or masked Self. I had always considered will, ego and concepts as comprising the conscious and the subconscious, and constituting Self. The idea of a division between Self and *ego* and Self and *will* had never occurred to me. Now, at last, I feel I know the meaning of I AM, the manifestation of God as Self in me."

There is every indication that this type of thinking will be attractive to Christian-oriented seekers in the Western world.

■ 7 ■

Much of PL's power lies in its ability to corroborate our deeper convictions and sustain our faith. Convinced that we are potentially better individuals than the ego we present to the world, we appreciate Patriarch Miki's admonition that the ego is an illusion and oftener than not a camouflage so stereotyped by custom and framed by society that we ourselves feel we must defend it as reality. But we know better. The onslaught of PL is directed inexorably at the unveiling of our divine Self mentally, physically, spiritually.

As to mind. After having been assured for generations that there are dimensions to our mental processes which we have never thoroughly explored or used, PL suggests that we begin to use them. How? By a conscious dedication to the Precept that every man's life is a series of self-expressions. By *unlimiting* ourselves, by casting off the restraining conditions that inhibit us, whether these have been induced by tradition or history or determined by religion or social sanctions.

There is a saying, "The fish that grows up in a bowl and is set free in the ocean will continue to swim in the circumference of the bowl until he has a change of mind."

Modern man now has the tools for mind-changing and mind-expansion. He has the example and help of cybernetics, of parapsychological discoveries, of brain wave control and memory control. The mind is a new frontier and PL recognizes this in its worldwide quest for the new man.

"It is in creativity," says Patriarch Miki, "that we discover the use of total mind function, and God is in the process as our unlimited Self."

This is the reason for the practical application of the Fine Arts Seminars. This is why the mind is sharpened by the *Tanka*, the world's oldest poetic art form, and extended by the insights into *Mishirase* and the finer grasp of *Mioshie*. From *Ikebana* to the creation of a Peace Tower the idea, *Makoto*, sets ajar the gates of perception. Many a PL follower begins his day with the Precept that man suffers if he fails to express himself and affirms before his *Omitama* that, "This is the day I practice the art of living!"

I dare say that today's youth, being what all of us were when we were young, dreamers and builders of dreams, contemplate what the world could be like if they had a chance to make it in their image. PL says that the image is realizable. Whatever is conceived can be achieved. Whatever is involved can evolve. This is the approach whether in clearing the atmosphere of pollutants and cleansing the earth of contamination, or clearing the mind of corruption, or ridding the world of strife.

"The quest for the seemingly impossible," says Oshieoya, "is for those who have resolved the possible."

On the sheer basis of the mental factor in man, PL creates a sense of kinship and fellow-feeling through the awareness of the hidden capability of mind.

As to the physical. PL believes that when people will not be moved by logical reasoning or by persuasion, then the only means for creating conviction is by commitment and performance. *Rensei*, as we have seen, is such an example. Through the fellowship of discipline, observer and participant are convinced of the wonder of physical well-being and true accomplishment. In *Rensei*, according to PL, an "original goodness" is restored to mankind.

Emphasis on golf and other sports, the attention given to preventive medicine and physical fitness in the hospital services, emphasize the fact that living in "perfect liberty" involves the inescapable responsibility for keeping the body healthy and strong. Here is the interplay between the physical man and the power of the mind, the psychosomatic balance constantly explained in ever so simple terms in the writings and references of Oshieoya.

"I knew a neurotic man," he says in one of his true-life parables, "who was usually in a fluctuating and irresolute state of mind and incapable of immediate decision, always at a loss what to do, which resulted in his physical illness. He never looked bright except when playing Ping-Pong!

"I said, 'You are not neurotic when playing Ping-Pong, are you?'

"He replied, 'That is right. And I cannot see why.'

158

"I said, 'It is because you are moving your arms and body while planning your attack.'

" 'Yes,' he said, 'I move before I think.'

"I said to him, 'As soon as you can act like that in everything, you will be rid of your neurosis and physical ills.'

"He shook his head. 'I would fail if I acted in everything as I do in Ping-Pong,' he murmured. 'If I fail and give my opponent a point, then I can always win it back.'

" 'You can win back in life, too,' I reminded him. 'As a matter at hand, a challenge in life is a Ping-Pong ball. The first thing to do is to strike. To strike and fail is better than to lose a point without striking.'

"When he was willing to admit that life *is* a game, he practiced quick decision in his life situations. It sometimes happened that too quick a decision brought about momentary failure, but when decisions were quick, a second trial could also be made quickly. He became more efficient in his work, he got over his habit of brooding, was cured of his neurosis and his physical health improved.

"One does not play a game with hesitation and irresolution. Neither should we play the game of life that way. Be decisive. Be sure. Body and mind must be coordinated."

The balance wheel is the spiritual nature of man.

You do not hear much about miracles or the magic of faith in PL, though deeply mystical overtones run through its history and though its leaders seem to be parapsychologically attuned in extraordinary ways, spiritual healing as practiced by most PL ministers also proves the presence of highly developed inner gifts. However, it is a PL conviction that the new age will prefer to call these phenomena normal and rational, contending that the better we get to know people on the spiritual level, the closer we come to the true person. The more the ego is effaced, the clearer becomes the inner man.

This is a way of saying that though you may not have

what you consider the capabilities you wish you had, you have the capabilities you *need*, and as you use them and appreciate them you will soon have the capabilities you wished for!

Many a PL member has told me that when the PL way is honestly lived, a "divine timing" takes hold of life. "When you catch on to the *Makoto*-style of living," one said, "you seem always to be in the right place at the right time. It is as though you are being moved about by a master chessman."

"I was looking for a job," a woman told me, "and I began doing *hosho* and living according to the PL principles in a special way. Almost immediately I got a job with one of the finest bakeries in Los Angeles. Here I was assigned to decorate prestige cakes and fancy baked goods because the chief decorator had suddenly quit. I had no training in cake decoration, but the manager came in and told me there was an order for a special cake with a lion decoration for a movie company. It was a rush order at that. I called my PL minister. 'Pray a special prayer for me and a lion!' I told him. Then I went to work. The design turned out so beautifully that those who saw the cake wanted others exactly like it!"

This, too, is *Makoto*. It is being motivated by our dreams, our wishes and our goals in life.

■ 8 ■

In my research among PL members I was given many explanations for the power of Perfect Liberty. "The power is in *Mioshie*," I was told. "It is in Oshieoya, in the Precepts, the Principles in *Oyashikiri*, in the *Omitama*, in the people."

But the most interesting answer came from a student at Ohio State who surprised me by reciting the Twenty-one Precepts. He had gotten hold of a book on Japanese religions, liked the story of PL and committed the Precepts to memory. This young man had his own unique answer to the power question.

"It goes back to the Patriarch," he said, "but his appeal is not in *him*, it is in *us*."

He was of the opinion that PL's influence lay in what Patriarch Miki *awakened* in each individual. Miki did not supply these potentials, he merely triggered them, stirred them up. This, the student proposed, is what religious leaders should do, arouse the sleeping giant of faith within oneself. The greatness of PL leadership, he felt, was not the superimposition of power, but its abstraction; not the injunction, "Look at us!" but, "Look at *yourself!*" Patriarch Miki was not saying, "Do as we say!" but, "Do your *own* thing!"

When I got into PL, or PL got into me, I found its power in *its ability to effect a philsophical cohesion with all faiths.* This quality of centroversion, that is, a tendency on the part of one religion to create unity in a self-creative way with all religions, was, to me, highly significant. Other religions, all the way from Hinduism to the Baha'i faith, had tried to make a synthesis of this kind meaningful and real, but PL had a somewhat different technique. Its Precepts reached out and "centroverted" every living faith.

For example, one morning I was reading portions of Emerson's treatise on "Art." I had read it before but now in the light of the PL Precept that "*Life* Is Art," its meaning substantially expanded. When Emerson said, "Because the soul is progressive, it never repeats itself. In every act it attempts the production of a new and fairer being," what was this but a commentary on the Precept that "Man's life is a succession of self-expressions," and "All things progress and develop?"

When the Transcendentalist Emerson declared, "The painter should give the suggestion of a fairer creation than we know," was this not the PL Precept that said, "Compre-

161

hend what is most essential?" And when he observed that, "Though we travel the world over to find the beautiful, we must carry it with us or we find it not," did not the PL Precept suggest this when it said, "All is a mirror?"

Obviously, when one searches for corollaries, they spring up everywhere in the mind of the imaginer. But it seemed to me I was finding them anew in old, familiar places, as everyone does who contemplates life in the light of the Twenty-one Precepts.

From the Sermon on the Mount, which clearly suggests that, "At every moment man stands at the crossroads of good and evil," to Modern Zen, which is based on the injunction to "Live in perfect unity of mind and matter," PL's power serves a catalytic purpose in bringing together values and ideas into a uniquely contemporary channel of understanding. *Perfect Liberty is the distiller of philosophies and religions which play upon the life of man, which have always done so, but have never until now been seriously unified in their essence and their common vital force.*

"We live together with many people," Oshieoya observes in his illustrative way, "and we owe much to people everywhere. The clothes we wear, the food we eat, and even the thoughts we think—surprising how much we owe to others! Yet the real meaning behind our saying that human life is relative is that each man should aim at self-expression on his highest level. He should aspire to such self-expression as no one else has ever attained."

That is the big idea, to know the full range of other men's aspirations and thoughts, to respect them, assimilate them, and then pass beyond them into one's own creative sphere. The creativity of human life *has* been given us for inspiration. We absorb it and then we go from there, as PL says, "To leave our own footprints in the world, footprints that can be distinguished from others, and that chart the challenge of something different and unique!"

Such is the power of PL and the dynamism generated at

Habikino, reaching out, embracing, influencing and synthesizing the aspirations men have always held. This is the focus on the new age and the goal of the Great Peace.

Where is the new man, the *Hito* man. Just beneath the surface of the human man, active within the worldly you and me, masked by ego. Efface the ego and he will appear.

To gain prestige, fame, wealth for wealth's sake, may seem all important for the outer man, but deep within he hears the whisper of the inner man, the true Self. In the midst of war, the true Self has long been saying, "Thou shalt not kill." At the height of world conflict, he has quietly affirmed, "Blessed are the peace-makers."

The NEW MAN, according to PL, advises that when opportunities and decisions are all about us, we should *"Comprehend what is most essential."* When things seem dark, we should *"Live radiantly as the sun."* When confronted by difficulties and challenges, we are urged to remember that *"LIFE IS ART!"*

If we must wait for the New Man to be *created* we may be too late, but if, as Patriarch Miki believes, he needs only to be *realized* since he already exists in each of us, we are in good time, and the power of Perfect Liberty is nearer and more universal than we think.